Dedication

Dedicated to everyone who has had his or her heart broken. May God heal the wounds of your heart. May you learn to trust and love again.

Elroy;
Thank you for your support. I pray you are blessed! May God prosper you in all you do!.
Blessings + love,
Dawodu

Table of Contents

Forward

Very seldom does a book arrest your attention to the point that you yield to its contents because the author's words present a mirror in which you can see yourself. Dr. Danon Carter accomplishes what many first-time authors only dream of and others are still in search of – a MUST READ BOOK.

Wounds of the Heart is a transparent book in which its author, Dr. Danon Carter, lays herself bare before the judge of truth. She bears all in this epic book and allows us to see the good, bad, ugly and most offensive occurrences of her life. As you read, you will sense yourself akin to a voyeur, as you walk with her through life's struggles moment by moment, and even so, you are acutely aware that this is exactly its purpose. By unveiling herself in such a public way, Dr. Carter both hooks and reels us into a place where Christ can be made known.

Wounds of the Heart is a necessary read for anyone who has ever experienced relationship failure and its destructive effects. In this book, Dr. Danon Carter addresses male/female dynamics and allows the reader to self-diagnose as they reason their way through the maze of relationship maturation.
Dr. Danon Carter's mature understanding of the Holy Scriptures does not allow wiggle room for private interpretation. As she chronicles some of her most difficult challenges, readers will find themselves re-evaluating their resolve to live for Christ.

Regardless of your religious background, creed, sexuality, or cultural experience – Dr. Danon Carter is sure to reach you with this book. For Church Leaders this book is a must read as it exemplifies how a leader should minister to those under the fragility of stress and duress.

Last, but not least, readers will enter a realm of personal introspection that will cause them to experience a greater awareness of faith and knowledge of how God expects us to practice biblical principles in any situation in which we find ourselves.

I highly recommend this book and am grateful to God for the struggles of Dr. Danon Carter. Surely her struggles were not in vain as every reader of *Wounds of The Heart* is sure to bless God for her obedience in publishing it.

Your Brother in the LORD,

Pastor Dion Evans

Author of the Book: 8 Giants to Defeat Before Facing Goliath
Twitter: @dionisms
FacebookFan Page: DION EVANS LIVE: TRUTH, RAW & UNCUT

Wounds of the Heart: A Heart Exposed

*I want to forget it ever happened but how can I erase
my heart?*
No matter what my mind tries to black out,
*My heart beats the thoughts of you right back to the
present*
I want to forget and forgive
Do I have to remember to forgive?
My mind and heart have a constant battle
While I stand on the sidelines, praying for control.
The bible says to control my thoughts...
But what about my heart?
*I want to forget in hopes of cleansing my heart of the
memories*
Is that so wrong?
My confidence is busted
*The choices I've made have led me down some dark
paths*
I don't trust myself.
My mind says one thing
My heart another...
Yet, neither are right
I can control forgetting, can't I?
How can I control what I feel?

"Do you want to be loved?" Such a peculiar
question, yet one I had to ask myself many times based
on situations I found myself in. Love is something we
all seek and in many ways, we all need to survive.
Challenges in our lives make love difficult and not as
appealing as love was meant to be. There are as many
things people do to be loved as things they do to avoid
love. Yet, love is still a need, a desire, a want, and a

necessity. Love is truly an interesting thing. We all want it but are often afraid to give it.

In my case, I was also afraid to receive love. I had all the wrong relationships… ones where true love could not be found. The hard part was removing from my mind all that I thought love to be, all that I experienced and called love, and all that I saw and thought was love. I had to come to know love based on the creator of love – GOD. God is not the love we experience from a man or a woman, mother or father, friend or any other relative, although God's love can be expressed through them and through us. We may not be worthy of God's love but God never said we had to be worthy to receive His love. Isn't that a blessing?

God says His love is unconditional. For us humans, this is hard to conceive. We think love has to have conditions or terms. "I love you if you do this for me"…. Or "I will no longer love you if you do this." We must be thankful that God does not assign terms to His love for us. What I learned through my trials and failed relationships was that God never left me. He held me through the years when I could not go on my own. He kept me when I was lost. He sustained me in my weakness. And God loved me when I did not feel I could be loved. I found God was always there even when I did not know it or could not feel it.

Have you ever found yourself in a relationship that you knew was wrong but you stayed… all in the name of love? Have you ever held on to a relationship when everything and maybe everyone was telling you to let it go? Have you ever felt so stuck in the pain of your decisions and choices that you did not feel you could recover? I've been there. I thought not only had I made bad decisions but also I wasted my life through the relationships I had. I did not feel I could ever get over the pain and hurt.

I am in a place in my life where I finally realize that everything has purpose. God does not waste one tear, one moment, one event. Once I awakened to this, my life changed and this book was born. But that was not until I went through many more valleys and more experiences I wished I could forget ever happened.

This book/workbook explores my personal journey of the pain of giving my heart away while allowing the love of God to heal the wounds of my heart. I had to submit to the process of healing. A heart hidden cannot be healed. A heart forbidden to feel cannot give love. Only a heart with wounds exposed can experience the healing of God.

I pray as you read my story you will *Take a Look in the Mirror* and answer the questions. Take some time to pray and record your thoughts while you allow God to search your heart for areas of deception and unhealed hurts. There may be some tough revelations about yourself, but don't give up! Take the time to allow God to heal you. I've also added a section on *Looking in the Rearview Mirror*, which provides insight into the chapter and what God revealed to me about the situation and myself. Each section ends with a prayer. You have plenty of room to write and reflect. May you begin your own journey of healing and draw closer to God in the process.

Soul Mate

When am I to have
That, which touches my heart
And turns it warm?
When am I to have
Him – who helps me
See me from all angles
When will it be my turn
To walk down the aisle
And say, "I do" forever
What is my destiny?
Is it not to be enjoined with one?
Spiritually & Physically?
What is my destiny?
If it is not to love
As I love myself
When am I to have
Completeness

"Please God, Bless This Mess!"

"You can make many plans, but the Lord's purpose will prevail." Proverbs 19:21

Christians often verge off the path of God and go create our own thing, and then ask for God's blessings. We often become impatient with God's timing or things don't look like what we expect, so we go our own way. When we get all messed up in our situation, we then ask for God's blessings. I know I have done this too many times to count. I've often found myself in a big mess with my lack of patience being my greatest fault.

This story begins with one of the biggest errors of my life! The only thing worse than getting involved with someone and realizing it is not a good fit is marrying someone and in less than 24 hours after saying, "I do!" realizing you just made the worse mistake of your life! "Please God, bless this mess" ... was all I could pray when I saw just how bad my "marriage" really was. I was indeed in a "mess". I was in one state and he in another. I had a "husband" but nothing about our marriage was normal. I don't recall a time when it ever was a "normal" marriage. At least not like ones I had seen from family and friends. I had to admit from the very beginning, I knew it was wrong, but still I went ahead with it, if nothing more than just to "save face".

Truth be told, there were warning signs before the big, "I do". There were glaring red, burning flags that I politely stepped over or went around as I pressed forward with what I thought I wanted. Why? Oh, for so many reasons. I was tired of being alone. I had blamed myself for many of my failed relationships and felt I needed to "fight" for this one, because maybe it was "just me". I had thoughts of "what if this is my last chance to get married and no one will ask me again". It had nothing to do with how I looked but how I thought about myself. I even thought, "What will my friends say?" I had brought this man around my co-workers, my friends, and my family.... I had to stay in this "mess", right? I convinced myself that if he stays, God must have sent him! I was so driven by my feelings of loneliness, shame, pride, worthlessness, and feeling I was incomplete without a man that I pressed on as if I needed to prove something by staying in my "mess"! Have you ever tried to make a relationship work just to prove you were not the problem?

So, here is my story or rather "the anatomy of my mess". I met this guy online. Finding or meeting up with men online became much easier than the club scene. The upside of online made it easier to create boundaries, with the added benefit of being able to communicate at length and "get to know" a person before meeting them. The downside was online also allowed people to misrepresent themselves. You could fall in love with an image of a person and not the real person. Overall, I thought my odds were better online then they had been otherwise.

This guy had a nice profile and his picture seemed to reflect a man concerned about his appearance. Initially, we exchanged emails and conversed that way for a while. Time passed with no contact and he seemed to call me out of the blue. He was in town and wanted to meet face-to-face. I began my departure off the path of God and onto my own path. I say this because I started doing things I had stopped doing or had never done previously.

I went with my son, then a toddler, to meet this strange man at McDonald's or somewhere that had a play area. Problem was it was getting late and places were closing, so I invited this stranger back to my place. He was nice enough, although he did not look anything like his picture. He made me laugh and seemed intelligent. We talked for hours till late in the night. See, prior to this, I had not invited a stranger in my home nor would I bring a man around my son. Let alone go out at night to meet a new person. Yet, common sense left me and I operated off of needs and desires. I even kissed him the first day. I recall getting on my knees and praying to God for this new "relationship" and for guidance after he left.

We spent the next several months meeting at my house, often during the workweek when I now took off time from work to be with him. We would spend hours talking and getting to know one another. To me, this was positive. We were not yet sexual but boundaries were definitely non-existent. I avoided all warning signs and pressed forward. I recall reading a devotional that stated, "Avoid addictive, obsessive relationships. If you are becoming increasingly dependent upon anything other than God to create a sense of wholeness in your life, then you are abusing your relationships." I heard it but did not see it for myself. I defended my relationship saying, "we clicked" from the very beginning. Our conversations were easy. We had a lot of things in common. And we were spending quality time learning about one another. Wasn't that different enough?

What should have been "warnings", I labeled as my "insecurities", so I prayed for strength and guidance, not that I was open to listening to anything different from what I wanted, which was a man to love me. I felt I had never been successful in relationships, so, I must break my destructive pattern recognize the warning signs, which were mainly pointed at me. I was pretty good at self-healing, at least I thought.

He said he had a roommate and no phone but I could page him and leave a message and he would call me. If I didn't hear from him for days, I would chalk it up to my own insecurities. I'd tell myself, "Everything is probably okay and I am worried about nothing" or "If he never calls me again, we were not meant to be." Then, I'd hear from him and all was right with my world again.

We'd spend time talking, playing games, drinking, and in a short time, having sex. We would discuss if our relationship could recover from "pre-marital sex" as initially, we both agreed celibacy was important if God was to be first in our relationship. He asked me about a month into the relationship if it was too early to get married. I told him there are things you need to know about a person before you can get married. He was silent for a while as if thinking about this too. All of these things told me this was different. *He* was different. I had finally found "the one"!

In a few short months, my job began talks of relocating me and in a whim, I asked this man to move with me and to my surprise he agreed. I had never lived with a man before, not even my son's father, so this was new to me. I thought I really had something special if this man would pick up and leave everything behind for me. What was his "everything"? He left the chauffeuring job but had his own business that was mobile, so he said.

His was estranged from his mother and sister. His father was deceased. No other family outside of his two kids, who lived with their mother. He'd still be close enough to go visit them, although I would never meet them. So many things were unknown about him even after hours and hours of conversation.

With my blinders on, I heard and saw only what I wanted to see and hear. I was in love. He professed his love to me and proved it by moving. I did tell him I did not want to live more than a year in sin and we would need to be married. He agreed and since we were already discussing marriage and our future, all was good.

> *I want the kind of love*
> *You find only in the movies*
> *You know the ones where the*
> *Main character finds love at first sight*
> *Where the courting is passionate and fun*
> *If there is such a thing…*

Previous relationships had made me withdraw into a shell. I had been hurt so many times yet I still desired a relationship and marriage. I just did not want to waste my time on someone who was not serious. In previous relationships, I would try to picture the man I was dating as my husband to give me a clue if it was meant to be or not. With one guy prior, I saw myself married to him but I also saw the things that would cause me pain or frustration and I ignored those things and stayed in the fantasy. With the new guy I saw the missing pieces and felt that was growth. I saw how to make myself whole. I saw how I did things differently, so of course this had to turn out differently! My prayers about him began on day one before I felt love knocking at my heart, that was different. Or maybe it was love that made me pray, or the desire for love. Yes, I desired and longed for love, real love. He even said the first "I love you" when we were on the phone one day. Doesn't that count?

Looking in the Rear View Mirror

The reality is I was in "my mess" for a few different reasons. One, I did not have the support of faith-based women to whom I could hold myself accountable. I had friends – good friends. I trusted them but did not know anything about accountability and how someone could speak into my life – the things God wanted me to hear. I was private. So, I did not share my personal life with others. That may also be due to I was in a place where all my friends and family lived in a different state. My sister lived a few miles from me but I did not share with her either. Know that the enemy can use isolation to attack your weak areas. God can also use isolation to draw you nearer to Him. Sin is a choice. And without a foundation, we can easily fail.

Second, I did not have a church home. I visited a church but had not made it my home. Thus, I was not under any spiritual authority. I did not have connections at the church where I would be missed if I did not attend one Sunday. I was not around true believers. This is not to say that a church will save you, as the teaching in the church have to come from God and His Word and there are many confused folks in the church. The point is I needed to be under regular biblical teaching and fellowship. This is huge. Much bigger than I ever realized but when you have never had this you don't know what you are missing.

Third, it is hard to discipline your flesh when you are not disciplined yourself. Plus, there are many things that can only be accomplished with the strength of God – meaning some things are beyond my best efforts. I was not in relationship with God. I had a religion and that is not the same. In a relationship, you spend time with a person. You get to know that person inside and out. You want to keep in contact and learn as much as possible to help build and nurture that relationship. That was not me. I had never been taught the difference between religion and relationship until much later in life after this blimp in my life.

Overall, we usually find ourselves in a "mess" when our choices do not align with God's Word. When we are moved by what our eyes see and let our emotions run us. When we decide we cannot share ourselves with others for fear of being judged, thus we don't even allow anyone to correct our thoughts. I've mentioned a few times the importance of validating everything against God's Word. I cannot stress this enough along with asking the Holy Spirit to confirm and reveal truth to you. In our vulnerability, we are easily deceived. Thus, we need to have real truth.

Read: Hebrews 4:12 & 13:7, John 16:7, 2 Timothy 2:15

A Look In the Mirror   **Date:**

1. If this were you, would you have called your mother or a trusted friend to come over while you entertained this man? How would you advise a friend?

_____
_____
_____
_____
_____
_____
_____

2. Consider your relationships. What steps have you taken to protect the purity of your relationships?

_____
_____
_____
_____
_____
_____
_____

3. In a desire for love or a relationship, what things have you done against your better judgment?

_____
_____
_____
_____
_____
_____
_____

God's Word:

"The fear of the Lord is the beginning of knowledge, but fools despise wisdom and instruction." Proverbs 1:7

Prayer:

Father, I pray that you will open my eyes and my heart to receive Your wisdom. Let my fear be in You and not in my desires. Lead me daily in Your instruction and on the path You have for me. Let me not get off track by the things or people that tickle my heart. Let my pursuit always be for You and not in man. Lord, send me godly mentors and friends to support me, correct me, and encourage me. I thank You for Your wisdom and instruction.

In Jesus' Name, I pray. Amen.

Notes:

_____
_____
_____
_____
_____
_____
_____
_____
_____
_____
_____
_____
_____
_____
_____
_____
_____
_____
_____
_____
_____
_____
_____
_____
_____
_____
_____
_____

Love My Way

I've often wanted love my way. I fell in love with the thought of love more than I fell in love. I was in love with the emotions more than the responsibilities and growing that comes with loving a person. Falling for someone who doesn't feel the same and cannot return the feelings seemed to be my preferred experience. Yet, I aimed to avoid vulnerability. The thought of love was often better than the reality.

REALIZATION

As it would be
I have fallen in love
With the feeling and not you
How could that be?

You possess so much of what
I thought I needed
Security, comfort, loving
And, yet, it's not what I needed

The thought was good
With its hopes of the future
Its commitment to end loneliness
Its promise to compliment my life vs. complicate it

So, could it be just a feeling
And not you
To warm my body, my soul, my mind
And touch my heart
To make me challenge myself
To give, to share, to change ME

> *And yet, I believed*
> *If I said those words*
> *You, soon, would echo the same*
> *But I must be deaf or you mute…*
> *I never heard them…*

  Why did I continually pursue love that only rejected me? I wanted love my way and on my terms and in my timing. Why didn't people give in to my rules? As I reviewed my life, I found I was often in the most emotionally destructive relationships. If it had only been one man that I held on to way past the expiration date, that may be excusable, but my pattern was holding on to something I should have released.

  I was a runner always seeking a reason to run. Well, not a physical runner but one emotionally. I kept my running shoes around my neck, laced, ready at the first signal of love. Always ready to run away from whatever mess I was in, usually one I created. Hindsight, I didn't think I was running on purpose. I had planted in my head the desire to run… every time the stress built to where I was having a hard time coping or felt like the feelings were becoming more than I could handle. I would put my running shoes on at the thought of something serious and at the slightest opening I was sprinting at top speed. I would rather run than stay and feel pain.

  I always wondered where the fear came from. I couldn't tell the difference between running, fleeting, and moving on. I could see the writing on the wall in relationships but would still stay… for a little while, then I would lace up again. I did not know how to heal and not repeat the same behavior over again.

I was not used to stability but more used to short-term relationships. Those I could start and stop when the pressure became too much. These relationships were obviously the unhealthy kind, ones that breed insecurity and distrust. Rejection seemed to fuel my pursuit. I mistakenly thought love, the love I chose, would bring me security, a sense of being. But even scared, I desired to live, love and be loved. So, I sacrificed myself.

I hurt in places I didn't want to know – yet, I didn't want to even acknowledge the hurt. Prior to my marriage, I had an emptiness that I tried to fill with people, alcohol, and sex, anything to ease my pain. I placed myself in situations to be rejected and abused, as somehow, I thought that was better than being alone.

I realized I was so broken and bruised from past relationships that I could not stand to be touched. A girlfriend and I could be talking and she may reach out to touch my arm as part of the conversation, but my arms were out of reach. A male friend of mine, whom I was actually interested in, walked up behind me and I jumped at his touch. Not in a "Wow! You scared me!" touch, but in an "Ugh! Don't touch me!!!" I equated a physical touch as entrance to my heart. My heart was bruised and covered with unhealed wounds. It hurt to be touched... so I created walls. Barricades... all to protect myself from any additional brokenness. I did not want to feel or be felt. This was from the same person who had led such a reckless life.

Sure, I read my bible but the words didn't take root because the soil was unhealthy. I sought fortune-tellers, horoscopes, and advice from all sources – anything that would come in alignment with my desires. Those that didn't, I ignored. I even cut ties with those who aimed to "correct" me... I felt they were preventing me from being in a loving relationship. Yes, I was confused and deceived.

See instead of looking for "warning signs", I went looking for confirmations that I *was* on the right path and that *this* relationship was meant to be. He had not mentioned wanting me to meet his kids or friends or anyone for that matter in a while. Yet, I opened myself up to so much with this new man based on what I thought was best for me. I placed him above God and felt I knew best what I needed in my life. And he was it! Sure I felt things may be going too fast, but that was just my fears talking. There was room to back out, as he hadn't financially committed himself, yet he still moved with me. And hearing him say he loved me and talk about our lives together after marriage... it was so vivid, so detailed, so specific... it *had* to be from God! So my "fears" turned into anxiousness for the future. It became an "exhilarating" experience where I would pray all would go according to God's plans, because surely God was in this!

We were both enthralled that we found each other and were progressing so smoothly. It was like a dream come true or better yet, a blessing! Doubt still hung around. We were talking marriage, although I hadn't met any of his friends or family. Yet, I could not imagine he could be so wrong, so fake that he could fool not just me but everyone around me. I felt I must be stupid, deaf, dumb, and blind to trust him and not fully know him... so I prayed. I began to realize the deeper I fell for him, the less I prayed for guidance. The deeper I fell, the harder it was to deal with any hint that we were *not* meant for one another. I did not want to hear God say he was *not* the man for me. I even felt guilty asking for forgiveness. So, I cast my anxieties aside and moved on.

I know someone reading this is thinking, "Really??? Come on! Wake up!!" but hindsight is always 20/20, perfect vision! While we are in the midst of our "mess", it looks good; it feels good... it is deceiving that way. And I was deep in it. I loved every minute of our time together. I loved the sinful moments. I was in love. I would constantly reflect and contemplate on what I thought was the attraction, the draw, what had me so enraptured, and if he and I were truly real. I would say, "If he's not real, he surely has gone out of his way to fool me. And I can't imagine someone putting their heart and their selves so far out there if it wasn't true." Nor did I want to ever imagine that it was all lies as I felt this would destroy my whole world.

We celebrated 90 days while laughing at all of the "rules" we made and subsequently broke. We were making our own "rules" and it felt good! We had our occasional challenges. He had difficulty finding a job in the new state. He drank out of control many times, showing no temperance. He liked my family but did not like the nurturing role I held in the family. I was typically the one everyone came to for help, including my mother. Family was important to me. So this was a big difference in our views and current family ties. In hindsight, he would have preferred if I were more like him without the family ties. But that was a small difference, right?

We worked through our issues pretty smoothly, although at times I felt he was irrational. I couldn't understand his point of view and he felt I did not honor him as the head of the household. Then one night he ended our relationship and walked out after a disagreement we had. Saying he did not want to be a burden to me, as I was too needed by my family. So my family could have me and I will be without a man. I could take care of everyone and no one would care for me or love me… is that it? I thought I had a man that would always be there for me… but I guess I was asking too much. I went from feeling I had the "greatest" love to nothing.

Could it all be a dream…
You and me, meeting by chance
The conversation that seemed to reflect I've known you for a lifetime
Or was it more of my inner heart's desire, a longing unfulfilled
Or even more, just a devilish spirit filling your head with my weaknesses
Did I lose myself in your kiss the very first night we met
Or was I just outside of myself daydreaming
About the feel of your lips on mine
I haven't quite figured it out yet…

The pain I felt at his departure was more than I could bear. I felt like all of his promises to me were lies. I felt all our time together was a dream and I was just waking up to only realize I was alone. I cried endless tears. My heart was broken once again. I did not want to believe it was all just a lie but that is what it seemed. Yet, all of these feelings and thoughts were only in a moment as he was back less than an hour later. Little did I know, this was only the beginning of his leaving and returning, the continual torture of my heart and feelings… still, I allowed it.

TIME AND AGAIN

You've disappeared
Time & time again

Fading…
Like a picture in the rain
What follows?
Anticipation, disappointment

You've like a bottle thrown out to sea
That keeps finding its way
Back to shore
When do you begin to sink
Fill… and take rest at the bottom

Or are you meant to constantly appear & reappear
Or does your presence hold meaning
As well as your absence

You're like the aftermath of a storm
Holding strong memories
Yet, through the destruction
There is always a fear of your return…

I took the apologies, the hugs, and the kisses and received him back into my heart because that was his place, right? Couples have disagreements right? He said all the right things. I was right, he was wrong. He said he needed me and told me how good I had been to him. I cried and held him, because I loved him too and I needed him. I did not want to lose him. He held me through the night and promised me he would not leave me again. I was emotionally exhausted but grateful we had surpassed this challenge. We committed to move forward without any grudges or bad feelings and not hold back on our love. And our "mess" continued.

Looking in the Rearview Mirror

There is a strange thing that happens when you have had bad relationships and you are hungry for a "good" one, you seem to take what you have and try to "make" it good. Truth is by the time I was in this relationship, I had seen enough of them fail that I had bought into the belief that "I" was the problem. I believed I gave up too soon. I believed I did not try hard enough or I was too selfish.

Truth is I was used to rejection and was willing to do what I could to avoid the feelings returning. I really thought I had something worth fighting for and was willing to change me to make it work. I wanted a "successful" relationship. And I did not want to feel like I wasted my time by investing in a failed relationship.

Truth is, I was not comfortable with me. I was tired of being single. I wanted a relationship. And I wanted a relationship to work. I did not know there was a purpose in my singleness. Even still, I truly believed if God did not send him away, then maybe it was His will. Yes, that was my false belief. I was willing to do what I could in the name of "love". Truth is we have free will and we are able to make our own decisions.

More truth, I was not healed from past relationships, thus should not have been in a new relationship. We often don't give ourselves time to heal from past hurts and we aim to cover the pain with a new relationship. Or we try other ways to heal ourselves. God is the true healer.

I thought if I prayed to God, He heard my prayers and would answer my prayers, in spite of my sin. Yet, sin can block our prayers. Sin keeps us from seeing reality. Sin keeps us from hearing from God. Yet, even in the midst of all of my mess, God is still God.

Isaiah 57:18-19 states, "I have seen his ways but I will heal him. I will guide him and restore comfort to him, creating praise on the lips of the mourners in Israel."

God still seeks to heal us in our pain, knowing our sin. He still aims to draw us nearer to Him and love us. Yet, He does not manipulate us. He does not abuse us. He does not force His way on us. He is the perfect gentleman. We have a choice. We can choose Him or we can choose the ways of this world.

But let me go back to the "Truth" of the previous chapter. There is a definite need to be in relationship with believers who can strengthen you when you are weak. Thus, you need friends strong in their faith and belief in God. If that had been the case for me, then I would have had someone to tell me I did not need to sacrifice myself for a man who was not walking with God.

Further, I did not have to tolerate a man who would continually come and go in my life. Since I did not set standards for what I would tolerate, the standards were set for me. As I continued to feed my flesh, my spirit was starved. The love I sought and fought to keep was not of God. Thus, I struggled.

Read: 1 Corinthians 13, Psalm 97:10, & Ecclesiastes 4:9-10

A Look in the Mirror   Date:

1. In what ways have you wanted love your way?

_____

_____

_____

_____

_____

_____

_____

2. What have you sacrificed of yourself to please someone else?

_____

_____

_____

_____

_____

_____

_____

3. What ill treatment have you allowed feeling you deserved it or did not deserve better?

_____

_____

_____

_____

_____

_____

_____

God's Word:

"So [Jesus] answered and said, "'You shall love the Lord your God with all your heart, with all your soul, with all your strength, and with all your mind, and [love] your neighbor as yourself.'" ~ Luke 10:27.

Prayer:

Father, Your Word says we are to love You with all our heart, with all our soul, with all our strength and with our entire mind. I ask You to help me love You more. Help me to love as You love. Help me to love Your way. Turn my heart and mind to You so I may love in pureness. Strengthen my flesh so I can stand in faith to You and not fall into the cravings of my flesh. I choose to love You, Lord, and Your ways. In Jesus' Name, I pray. Amen.

Notes:

_____

_____

_____

_____

_____

_____

_____

_____

_____

_____

_____

_____

_____

_____

_____

_____

_____

_____

_____

_____

_____

_____

_____

_____

_____

_____

_____

What's Love Got to Do With It?

THIS LOVE

I feel strongly – this love
It takes me away at times
Soaring to levels of intense satisfaction
And sometimes falling to the point of a question
At moments it bombards me with tears
Without justification or meaning
But every second it still exists
Holding tightly to my warm heart
It breaks me into reality
Shocking the breath from my lungs
Making me accept these emotions
Its life course seems to outlive my own
Overpowering my mind with its deepness
Causing at times wounds to reopen
Pain to creep into my veins
Pinching my nerves with every heartbeat
But then it soothes – calming my body
Relaxing my soul, while whispering, "There's more."
At times I tell it to go away
To plague someone else – run them
But then it refuses and promises to stay
Other times I welcome it with open arms
Pleading with it never to leave
To constantly show its face
Reassuring me it is still there
I feel I am running with it
But in transposition – it is running with me
Taking me for a ride I'll never forget.

I am slowly finding that love has a lot to do with it. When the feeling of love is involved, we often do crazy things. It is a heart thing that attaches us to that of which we love. And for the sake of love, we go places we may not go otherwise. Yet, our definitions of love are not often based on how God defines love. The whole concept of love will get us in situations we would swear we would never be in… yet we may find ourselves there, all in the name of love.

Once you have experienced something painful, you would hope to recognize the pattern to avoid falling into the same situation again. Sometimes this is not as easy as it should be. Signs may look different, the faces can change and even the outside environment may look altogether new. But just when you think you are over something, you find there is something so familiar about this "new" thing.

The question arose, "What have we gained by living together before marriage?" As our relationship continued to have its challenges, I wondered if he was struggling because we did not follow the right steps. See, I did not view myself as struggling. He was the man. He was to be the spiritual leader in the house. I felt I had gained support from having him with me 24/7 – physically and emotionally, and even spiritually, as I was definitely praying more. I trivialized the experience saying it was not so bad to live together and plan our future as a married couple versus dating and sleeping around. I understood both options may be considered bad but I succumbed to that I was praying for guidance, not listening, but praying nonetheless.

Conviction came in many forms and from many mouths, but the heart wants what the heart wants, right? Even my dreams warned me… but forward, I continued. I loved him. He loved me. So even the "wrong" looked right. We progressed and soon he proposed on both knees and of course I accepted… all to make my dreams come true, I guess. We have to remember the enemy also knows our dreams.

This was the plan and all was in order. We had a two-day engagement party with all my family and friends.... I still had not met anyone from his family, although he did introduce a friend and his wife. I was happy with the one connection and comforted that someone from his past confirmed my existence in his life. I began planning a destination wedding. I was also paying for it, as he still was not working. I hoped the lure of the tropical would bring our friends and family to support and celebrate with us.

Four months later, my happiness began to slowly unravel as he once again left, this time to settle some legal matter. You must understand, his "leaving" was not "I'll be gone a few days." It was packing up as if he would never return. He claimed he was turning himself in and would be incarcerated for a time. He claimed it was child support related. I really had no idea what this could be even though I thought it was good that he was doing the "right thing".

> *My happiness has left me*
> *The memories cannot fade as easy*
> *As water evaporating on hot cement*
> *My smile is turned down*
> *As I fight for my sanity*
> *I long to touch someone to touch you*
> *To know it is all real….*

I was still unsure about the nature of his leaving and why I had not heard from him in days. My fear of our love ending was becoming more real with each day of his absence and no contact. I hurt in places only love could touch. Yet, I knew if love never touched those places again, my survival was questionable. I prayed for love not to leave me, not to fool me… not again. God did bless this love, right? I felt this pain was a result of my misplaced faith. I prayed to know God and to hear His voice as clear as a bolt of thunder in the middle of the night. I needed that type of clarity, as I feared I would not hear otherwise.

I reached out to the only friend of his I had met and he expressed his concern also. I prayed for him to come "home" as I needed him and missed him so much. With each day of no contact, I began to worry so I started some digging as initially I felt I did not fully hear or recall where he was going. I checked all the jails in his area, and there was no record of him. I checked his email (his email was on my account)… yes, I was desperate for answers.

From this point on, truth would continually be exposed little by little. I found he had been lying the whole time. He was dating other women on the side. I realized the only thing I was good for was giving him a home for free, since he still was not working. I had heard the warnings and yet, once again I ignored them. I wasn't sure how much more it would take for me to learn my lesson. So, thought it best to heed the truth in front of me… he was gone, not where he said he was, and the emails revealed he had not been faithful. Thus, I called off the wedding, changed the locks on the house as well as changed the codes on the alarm, just in case he did come back. I was done and moving on.

What I found most interesting is that he had been cheating and accused me of the same. So you know what they say about a woman scorned? I changed his home page on his email to add some truth to the man he was. I sent out emails to the ladies he had been in contact with to let them know what type of man they were dealing with and that up until that moment, they were involved with a man who was engaged. Feeling accomplished, I then sent out an email canceling the wedding. I couldn't imagine him coming back to the house, after he found out I knew about his lies, although he had left a few of his things there. Maybe he wanted to get caught. Whatever the reason, I was done.

Less than a week later, he turned up with more "forgive me" and "I was scared", and how he really was in jail. And "please forgive me", etc. He begged me to talk to him face to face. I succumbed and he came back to the house and back into my life. Truth be told, I wanted to save face. I did not want to admit that we were not the "perfect" couple. I still wanted my tropical wedding. The wedding was back on and we were back on track for a lifetime of love. As a couple, we attended his friend's wedding. I sat next to a guy who ushered and when I introduced myself, he knew me. My fiancée had told him about our engagement, our pending wedding, and me. For some reason, I felt validated.

Looking in the Rearview Mirror

God's Word says in 1 Corinthians 13: 4-7 (The Message version), "Love never gives up. Love cares more for others than for self. Love doesn't want what it doesn't have. Loves doesn't strut, doesn't have a swelled head, doesn't force itself on others, isn't always 'me first', doesn't fly off the handle, doesn't keep score of the sins of others, doesn't revel when others grovel, takes pleasure in the flowering of truth, puts up with anything, trust God always, always looks for the best, never looks back, but keeps going to the end."

I loved the concept of love. I loved the promises of love. I loved "Love" more than I did the reality of my experience. Understand, as I have learned, God will allow us to make our own choices and decisions – even if that leads us off the path He has for us. His grace allows us to experience the consequences to draw us back to Him. 1 John 4:8 states, "God is love."

The love I had for my ex and he told me he had for me was not this type of love. I may have thought by continually accepting him back in my life that I was demonstrating unconditional love but really, what I was demonstrating was a lack of love for myself. I did not think I was worthy of more and that I had to just tolerate his unfaithfulness. His love for me was not the 1 Corinthians love. He used the word "love" to keep my heart turned towards his because I believed love should be forgiving and tolerant.

Truth is, I had a relationship with a guy, when I was in High School, who was 3 years or so older than me. My mom liked him but was not so happy that he was older than me. He, too, would disappear for weeks at a time and then show up again. I somehow thought this was normal. Eventually, I found out he was living with a woman and would spend his "off" time with me. I tolerated it for a year or so until I couldn't take it anymore during one of his absences. Bottom-line, we all, male and female, have to look at the unhealthy patterns in our lives that cause us to continue to make poor decisions in our adulthood. We may make choices based on past hurts, seeking to prevent further hurts, or we may make choices consistent with experiences in our past.

Another truth is often when presented with the truth we may choose to live in denial. God often provides us with the truth and then sits back and waits for us to choose what to do with the truth. We can ignore it or we can change it into what we call truth. In my situation, I had the truth but did not want to believe that his love was not "true". My desire for love was greater than my desire for truth. Thus, I had to live with my decision and face the hard truth of my situation.

Read: 1 John 4:7-9, Galatians 5:6-10 (The Message version) and Romans 5:8

A Look in the Mirror **Date:**

1. For the sake of "love" what have you allowed?

_____
_____
_____
_____
_____
_____

2. What decisions have you made based on emotions?

_____
_____
_____
_____
_____
_____
_____

3. Have you ever chosen to stay with someone because you did not think anyone else would love you?

_____
_____
_____
_____
_____
_____
_____

God's Word:

"I will love You, O Lord, my strength. The Lord is my rock and my fortress and my deliverer; My God, my strength, in whom I will trust; My shield and the horn of my salvation, my stronghold." ~ Psalm 18:1-2

Prayer:

Father, I need You as my rock and my fortress and my deliverer. As my rock, You keep me steady and help me to stand. As my fortress, You protect me from all harm. You provide me a hiding place, a place to run to when things of this world are too much for me. And as my deliverer, You rescue me from trouble. You save me from my enemies. You forgive my sins. Lord, I recognize in all of this, in my weakness, I can cause myself to fall. I may need protection from myself. And I may need You to rescue me from *me* and my decisions. I thank You that I can put my trust in You, my Shield, my Horn of Salvation, my Stronghold. Please hear my prayer, in the Name of Jesus, I pray.

Notes:

_____

_____

_____

_____

_____

_____

_____

_____

_____

_____

_____

_____

_____

_____

_____

_____

_____

_____

_____

_____

_____

_____

_____

_____

_____

_____

_____

_____

Broken, Bruised, and Overused

What have we become?
You and I
Besides unhappy
Each experiencing some type
Of loneliness without the other
Yet fighting the feelings
Only to be plagued with the need
To be with the other

So, full of a renewed hope that maybe he wasn't all that bad and could be redeemed, we spent time talking and trying to repair the damage only for him to leave six weeks later. This time I came home from work one day and he was just gone. I didn't get a chance to say goodbye. And just like that, I was back in the pits. It seemed he used this "leaving" to toy with my feelings. He seemed to be running from the commitment, yet I could not understand why he continued to return.

He left a long message on the house voicemail with some unexplainable reasons I could not comprehend… something about claiming to seek employment elsewhere and to "repair" himself and get back on his feet because we could not begin a marriage like this. I could halfway understand that not working was stressful for him and he wanted to provide for his kids and me. Though I didn't want to make it all about me. I knew their birthdays were coming. Yeah, it all made sense. Still, I was broken and hurt all over again. I was lost. I prayed for God to bring him back, let this not be the end of us. I dreaded mourning something that was already feared to be unreal.

As the days passed and I did not hear from him, I feared he would never return. The tears stopped and I began praying for God to carry me through this... I became numb. Yet, I had not given up hope. Hope for what, I'm not sure. I trusted God and felt if it was to be, it would be, either way, God's will. I found little support in my situation. Well, not the support I wanted anyway. I wanted to be encouraged to stay in my mess. My heart was broken; I wanted comfort, not conviction. I did not want someone to be happy that he was gone, yet again. I did not want to believe I had fallen for this kind of "love". I did not want to be judged.

Can a love that felt so good, so real disappear so quickly. Have warm words melted away like thin air? All the promises... I let myself believe again – just false. I questioned everything – was anything real or was it all a big bad dream? How many others did I bring into my dream? I even questioned my destiny. Maybe he was right and we couldn't recover from the lies. Maybe that was only for "true" love and God may not have blessed our love.

Out of all of my blessings, I still felt punished when it came to love. I feared I loved the wrong men... forever allowing people to get too close to me where I could get hurt. Maybe I was not meant to be loved? To marry? Maybe I was meant to be alone. I felt this was the closest I would ever be to marriage and happiness. I wasn't sure I would ever get that close again. No, I couldn't allow myself to ever get that close to someone again. It was too painful. I felt broken, betrayed, alone, shamed, lonely and angry. Did I see this coming and just ignored it? Probably. I just did not want to believe it or allow my words to become his actions. I even wondered if I was giving up too soon or too late. So, I gave it to God... again.

With my home life in disarray, my work performance suffered. I was torn. I was hurt. I had to pick myself up. I determined "I am redeemed." I did not have to wait on redemption; Jesus already gave it to me. This phase of days in my life was only small troubles, I told myself. I would not allow my enemies to bring me down. Hadn't I been through even worse heartbreaks and recovered? Yes, I had to encourage myself through my situation.

Then in my brokenness, God returned him to me almost a month later. We talked and had more of the "I love you", "I missed you", "I'm sorry for hurting you" conversations. He confessed he still wanted to marry me. And I believed him. I needed to believe. I had to ask myself if I was willing to overlook his lies and infidelities. Or was it just my insecurities that caused me to believe he was untrue? I was tired of failed promises of forever. I wanted those promises of forever till the end of time.

> *To be strong*
> *When all inside you*
> *Wants to break down*
> *To do right*
> *When the definition is unclear*
> *And right proves harder*
> *To smile*
> *When deep inside*
> *The pain is unbearable*

When he left me the last time and after the engagement party, the invites were already out. I couldn't call off the wedding. No, it was too late. What would people think? Many of the people I was around and worked with had never seen me with a man as I had kept my private life private… before him. They saw me as this strong, successful, single black woman. I had always made good choices – at least that is what people thought. What would they think now? Yes, unfortunately pride was a driving force for continually allowing this man to come back to me. I was driven by the fear of being alone. I feared people knowing that he did not want me.

I was so full of pride that I did not want to cancel the wedding and tell others what happened. The thought of feelings of emptiness without this man overwhelmed me, and to top it off, I had ended my celibacy with him before we got married. I let him move in with my son and me. How could I walk away??? I felt I had so much to prove. The reality sunk in, the weight of my sin and the consequences of my decisions were huge … this was my life.

I hated "needing" someone. I only wanted to "need" God and His Son, Jesus, and to be a faithful servant. I wanted to be strong spiritually but my flesh was weak. I wanted to be strong and resist temptation. I did not want to be needy. Reality was I was a flawed human who operated by her heart instead of her head.

Looking in the Rearview Mirror

I was broken by past relationships. I was bruised by rejection and false claims of love. I was overused in continually giving my heart to those undeserving. Yet, I continued to subject myself to the pain. I continued to place myself in situations of hurt. I continued to believe the best while experiencing the worse. This is not to say we do not forgive and love. I was just moved more by my heart than I was by God's heart.

Reality, I justified his actions. I justified my needs. I justified my mess. It was much easier to say I was unworthy then to fully believe this relationship was not meant to be.

What I learned is when someone wants to leave – let them go. You cannot force someone to stay. You have to believe there is purpose in both staying and leaving. Trust God. Don't mourn what God removes from your life. I wanted a man above my relationship with God. God wanted me.

God teaches me that He will remove any idol in my life that tries to take His place. His is a jealous God and will not allow us to place others or things above Him. And through His grace, He provides so many opportunities and ways out of the situations we find ourselves in… but we still have a choice.

It is also important to recognize the patterns in our lives. My pattern was staying when I needed to leave or holding on to things or people way beyond the expiration date. I, often, stayed within my own patterns of abuse, as I did not seem to know anything different. So, I stayed with the familiar.

My pride played a big role in my decisions. I did not want to believe that an educated women as myself would fall for the "okie doke", as my mother would say. Funny thing is, in my head, I *always* made wise decisions but in reality, my men choices were seldom wise.

The bible says, "When pride comes then comes shame; but with the humble is wisdom." ~ Proverbs 11:2. And Proverbs 16:18 states, "Pride goes before destruction and a haughty spirit before a fall." Thus, we must always check the motive behind what we do. Are we seeking approval of others? Are we more concerned about what others will think? Or how this situation will make us look? This is all pride.

Surround yourself with wisdom. Allow God's Word to speak to you. Don't allow the reality of a situation to isolate you from others.

Read: Deuteronomy 8:19 & 28:13-15, Psalms 86:7-9 and Galatians 4:7-9.

A Look in the Mirror   **Date:**

1. Have you ever feared being alone?

_____

_____

_____

_____

_____

_____

_____

2. Have you ever covered up emotional or physical abuse for the sake of keeping others from knowing what you were going through?

_____

_____

_____

_____

_____

_____

_____

3. What have you allowed for the sake of staying in a relationship?

_____

_____

_____

_____

_____

_____

_____

God's Word:

"Cause me to hear Your loving kindness in the morning, for in You do I trust; Cause me to know the way in which I should walk, for I lift up my soul to You. Deliver me, O Lord, from my enemies; In You I take shelter. Teach me to do Your will, for You are my God; Your Spirit is good. Lead me in the land of uprightness. Revive me, O Lord, for Your name's sake! For Your righteousness' sake bring my soul out of trouble. In Your mercy cut off my enemies, and destroy all those who afflict my soul; For I am Your servant."
~ Psalm 143:8-12

Prayer:

Lord, just as Your Word says in the Psalm above, I ask that You cause me to hear Your loving kindness in the morning and throughout the day and into the night. Cause me to know the way in which I should walk and keep my feet on the path You have for me. Let Your mercy overflow in my life as You keep my enemies at bay and preserve my soul for Your name's sake. I want to serve You, Lord, please be my guide and my teacher. I pray in Jesus' name. Amen.

Notes:

_____
_____
_____
_____
_____
_____
_____
_____
_____
_____
_____
_____
_____
_____
_____
_____
_____
_____
_____
_____
_____
_____
_____
_____
_____
_____
_____
_____
_____

Ask and You Shall Receive

So I accepted him back, again and again and continued with the wedding. I accepted his apologies and reasons for "leaving". He convinced me he was stronger and ready to be the "man" I deserved in a marriage. Yes, he said all the right words to re-open my heart to him. Thus, the wedding planning was in full swing. The trip paid for and time scheduled. He agreed to introduce me to his kids. His "job" now required him to travel frequently, thus it was now expected that he would be gone days at a time. At least this time, I would know where he was and hear from him regularly.

He would come in town frequently but often his attitude was easily roused. He became easily agitated and often verbally angry. His anger would destroy our time together and it was often the smallest things. We even argued through email. Then, he would apologize and we would move on. Maybe it is just me and my insecurities and lack of trust. Maybe I needed to change and not him. Oh and the famous, "No one has ever loved me like this before" and "maybe he will change once we are married" came into play. I may have even thought that I could change him. As the wedding neared, I put all fears aside and pressed forward. Things calmed down and we were on our way to the destination wedding in the Caribbean.

Two days before the wedding, my fiancé's blood sugar crashed and I had trouble waking him. I gave him glucose tablets and checked his blood twice before he was fully conscious. If that wasn't enough, this happened again after the wedding while still on our honeymoon. I awoke to him shaking and could not get him conscious. This time, his levels were in the teens.

He was going into diabetic shock. I gave him glucose tablets and sugar cubes and when those did not work, I prayed for God to save my husband and not to take him so soon. I had to call the resort nurse who gave him a shot of glucose to bring his levels up. We checked his levels again and he was only in the mid- twenties, but he was conscious. I was thankful.

Not only was he having medical issues, his attitude had dramatically changed once the "I Do's" were said. Less than 24 hours after I said, "I Do", I was awakening to the realization of the mess I had gotten myself into based on what I thought was "love". He became obsessively possessive and protective of me, thinking even the waiters were trying to hit on me. I did not know what to make of it but knew I had made the wrong decision. I had so many failed relationships and I was determined to make this one work.

Yes, he had changed once we were married but not for the good. My reality was I was married to a man but had never met his family or kids, only a couple of his friends. My bottom line was that I now had a husband I barely knew and I felt deep inside this marriage was a mistake. I was stuck with a commitment, a vow I made to God in marrying this man. What a mess! Nothing is worse than knowing your decisions and choices have gotten you into a situation that is hard to get out of ... especially without breaking vows and promises to God. All I could pray was "God, please bless this mess!"

After the wedding he stopped traveling and stayed home. The first two months were okay but soon things became challenging again. I had quit my job a month before the wedding and had taken another job that would begin a few months later. The job required travel and that was a real strain on the marriage, although both decisions were made with his approval and support. He was not working and served as the caretaker for my son while I traveled. He was supposedly looking for work but only God knows what he was really doing.

We would argue about all kinds of stuff. He would pick fights – mostly while I was traveling. It was just the stress I needed while away from home and while he was there with my child. He would often leave the day I flew back into town. I never knew if he would be home when I returned or if he was "visiting his kids". I was dealing with my own insecurities because I had not completely forgotten his indiscretions. He tried to convince me that all of his indiscretions were before the marriage and I shouldn't hold that against him. He told me love requires trust... so I should trust him, if I really loved him. So, maybe it was just me.

Ten months into the marriage, I changed jobs again and was forced to relocate. We were struggling financially - especially with only me working, so he agreed that this was the right decision and again fully "supported" me. We agreed the move was the best thing for us. Yet, he never moved. When the furniture arrived from the movers, I found many of his things were not included. He continually promised me he would be moving soon, he just had to finish some things and wanted to be near his kids as long as possible.

"Soon" never happened. He would come once a month or so then it became every few months, I eventually lost track. I came to the point where it was harder to be with him than to be without him. I spent our first year anniversary alone. I don't believe he even remembered it. I received a couple of e-cards and empty promises but that was it. This only served to add to my regrets.

I felt so cheated. This was not like any marriage I had ever dreamed about or any that I knew of. I couldn't believe "this" was what I had held out all these years for... "This" was what I so desired. "This" is what I sinned for and cast away my values for! I never had a normal marriage where two people live under the same roof or where arguments turned into silent treatment in the same house, the same bed. I was so torn. I was stuck in a marriage that never should have happened.

A Dream of a Troubled Soul
I dreamed a dream that was full of you
It showed me months of experiences I shared with you,
It told the story of a troubled soul
That yesterday had answers, but today no more...

I prayed and prayed for God to heal my marriage. I prayed for God to change him. God answered me and told me not to worry about what he was doing but to focus on HIM and for me to honor my vows to God. One of the hardest things I had to learn in my marriage was honoring God above all else and being faithful to God, even when I felt wronged. God expects us to look to Him in every situation and to trust Him even when we don't think we are treated fairly. See, although My husband had a responsibility to God, so did I. Regardless of what he was or was not doing, God expected me to honor Him. God wanted my heart - regardless of the situation. So, I gave my marriage to God. I joined a church, got involved with a praying wives' small group. I committed to honoring my vows and I truly learned to submit. I pressed in to God and He covered me with an indescribable peace.

Looking in the Rearview Mirror

Matthew 6:21(the Message version) – "Don't hoard treasure down here where it gets eaten by moths and corroded by rust or - worse! – stolen by burglars. Stockpile treasures in heaven, where it's safe from moth and rust and burglars. It's obvious, isn't it? The place of your treasure is the place you will most want to be, and end up being."

My "treasure" was in a dysfunctional relationship. My "treasure" was in a marriage void of God. I placed more value in the relationship with man then I did in my relationship with God.

Reality, a marriage without God is not a marriage. Since God was not our foundation, our marriage was on sinking sand. See, I had a vision of what I wanted and what I thought marriage would be but there was no biblical foundation. We had veered so far off the path of God that common sense was long gone.

Second, I did not have a mentor. I did not have anything to compare to or to use as a model for my marriage… I just knew this was not it and it was not right. I did not come from a family where everyone stayed married. I did not know the backstories or had ever heard of challenges like I had experienced in my marriage. I just believed when two people committed to one another in God's name, it was for keeps and that both parties would work it out. And I never expected the honeymoon phase to end so soon.

The couples I did know had marriages that lasted much longer than we had and had happier times, so I thought since I was never told any different. Not to say my friends needed to share all the details of their marriage with me, I just did not have anyone to tell me any different… and I am not sure I ever asked.

Third, sometimes the things we want are not good for us – yet, in spite of that, we still desperately pursue these things believing they will make us better eventually. Submitting to God's will means we release hold of everything we think we want and cling to what He wants. That requires us to hear from God and seek Him to know His will.

Sacrifice is difficult and submission is even harder. Sin clouds our vision. It can distort the reality of our situation. Once emotions are involved, we become "committed" to the sin, as to stop would alter the situation and possibly spur more negative consequences. Thus, once I had rationalized myself into this marriage, I did not see how to stop sinning would have made things any better after the fact (me – rationalizing). My blinders were this "love" and I felt I loved him. He would profess his love dozens of times throughout the day – so, I thought this would eventually help the marriage. But saying you love someone is not enough. There must be action. The love must be healthy. The love must reflect God.

Read: Deuteronomy 4:29 & 30:16-18, Psalm 20:4 & 81:11-13, and Ephesians 4:7-19

A Look in the Mirror   **Date:** _____

1. Have you ever wanted a relationship that seemed to be outside of God's will?

_____
_____
_____
_____
_____
_____
_____

2. Have you ever wanted something so badly that you compromised your values to attain it?

_____
_____
_____
_____
_____
_____
_____

3. Have you ever asked and prayed for something only to realize what you wanted was not what you needed?

_____
_____
_____
_____
_____
_____
_____

God's Word:

"Ask, and it will be given to you; seek, and you will find; knock, and it will be opened to you. For everyone who asks receives, and he who seeks finds, and to him who knocks it will be opened."
~ Matthew 7:7-8

"Trust in the Lord, and do good; Dwell in the land, and feed on His faithfulness. Delight yourself also in the Lord, and He shall give you the desires of your heart. Commit your way to the Lord, Trust also in Him and he shall bring it to pass." ~ Psalm 37:3-5

Prayer:

Lord, Your Word says if I ask, what I ask will be given to me. Your Word also says I should delight myself in You and You will give me the desires of my heart. Forgive me, Father, for the times I have desired things outside of You and Your will. Forgive me for the times I have asked for things that didn't glorify You. Help me to trust in You more Lord and to feed on Your faithfulness. I choose to commit my ways to You Lord and trust that You will bring it all to pass according to Your will and Your Word. In Jesus' Name, I pray. Amen.

Notes:

_____

_____

_____

_____

_____

_____

_____

_____

_____

_____

_____

_____

_____

_____

_____

_____

_____

_____

_____

_____

_____

_____

_____

_____

_____

_____

_____

_____

_____

_____

_____

Walk by Faith

And Jesus said, "Peace. Be still."

Faith is the foundation we walk on... it is what wakes us up in the morning and keeps us going through the day.
Faith is what keeps us believing even when things look bleak.
Faith is what encourages us when we've had a bad day... as our faith helps us press into tomorrow.
Faith is what allows us to cross over and under bridges, as we know man fails but God doesn't
Faith is what builds us up when we are torn down.
Faith is what fills us when hope seems lost.
That same faith can change what seems hopeless into something hopeful
Faith is what heals the broken and causes us to love once again, when we thought we never could.
We have faith that God hears our prayers.... because He answers so many of our unspoken ones.
We have faith that God is in control as we can think we know but still be confused on what direction to go.
Faith is that unexpected phone call, that kind word from a stranger,
Those unmet needs – met.... all because God loves us.
If you don't have faith.... what do you have?

I used to think that a ring on someone's finger meant someone loved him or her. It used to make me feel good that no matter how good or bad someone looked or acted, there was someone who committed his or her love to them. Now, I realize a ring is nothing without action and faith behind it. It is like wearing a cross because it is a nice piece of jewelry and not because of its significance of Jesus dying on the cross for our sins.

The commitment must be eternal as God's sacrifice of His Son was for us. There must be faithfulness – not just to each other but also to God. Everything must be done to give God the glory. Everything must be done in full obedience to Christ. Everything must be done through the guidance of the Holy Spirit. These things are not seen in a ring... so I began to pray.

Initially, I prayed for God to fix him. Change him. Fix my marriage. The worst part was my husband knew the Word but did not live the Word. He could quote scriptures and have a very deep conversation on the things of God but did not walk in the ways of God. I asked God, "Do You see what he is doing? Lord, he is not here with me. He is not being the husband You said husbands should be. Do something Lord!" God reminded me to be faithful to Him and He would handle my husband. So I prayed.

Dear Lord,
I have a burden on my heart. My husband is separated from me. He is living and doing things unknown to me. I am not comfortable not knowing – yet, I don't think I would be comfortable knowing. Lord, I confess, I don't fully trust my husband. I feel abandoned by him. I know You are here with me Lord and I am thankful You are. I also know I can come to You and discuss my feelings of fear and concern, especially where my husband is involved. I want to love him wholly. I don't want to have any bitterness in my heart where he is concerned. I also don't want to look to him for things I get from You, Lord. I just never imagined my marriage would be like this. I understand there are ups and downs (to say the least)

and I wasn't expecting an easy ride. I just would like to have some sort of normalcy to my life. My husband and I under one roof, sharing our ups and downs together. I pray Lord you will show me what I need to do to aid this in happening. How can I be part of the reconciliation?

Dear Lord,
I continue to struggle with trusting my husband. I am having a hard time understanding why he is not here yet. It bothers me greatly and as the months pass on, I am feeling more and more that he doesn't want to be here. I don't know if I can believe what he says to me.
I know I can't blame You, Lord, for something I messed up by not following the steps You gave me. I only ask that You direct me from here. Lead me to the scriptures that will give me peace, comfort, and guidance.
I am lost. I am dependent on You, Lord, to show me the way. Take control of my thoughts and actions that are against Your will. I need Your help Dear God.

Dear Lord,
It's me again! I am still struggling with trusting my husband. I am struggling with feelings of insecurities and loneliness. I admit I don't like being alone. I also admit I want to give up often… it is easier than fighting and the unknown. I know a big part of the "unknown" is having faith and faith does not come by sight. My thoughts are uncontrolled, which impacts my dreams. My love for my husband is true. You know that. I just don't like this separation. I don't see a light at the end of this tunnel. Where I am uncomfortable being alone – my husband seems to thrive off of it. How can we ever come together again? I know through You all things are possible and I know You alone control the gates of what comes and goes in my life and I trust Your judgment.

*Help me to have peace **about** my marriage as well as **in** my marriage. I pray Your will be done in this marriage and in our lives – not my will.*

I am going to make a strong effort to be positive, to look to edify, and to be more supportive. Please keep me in this mission. I am going to focus on putting my trust in You and not in man.

I sometimes feel like I am a hair from falling apart. I have no idea what direction I am heading.

I pray for Your guidance, direction, discernment, chastisement as well as encouragement. Please work in me a work that gives You the glory and honor.

Lord, it is hard at times to pray for my husband. I confess my anger, hurt, unforgiveness, disappointment, resentment, and hardness of heart towards my husband. Forgive me and create in me a clean heart and a right spirit before You. Give me a new positive, joyful, loving, forgiving attitude towards my husband. Where he has erred, reveal it to him and convict his heart about it. Lead us both through the paths of repentance and deliverance. Help me not separate from him emotionally, mentally, or physically due to unforgiveness. Where either of us needs to ask forgiveness of the other, help us to do so. If there is something I'm not seeing that is adding to the problem, reveal it to me and help me to understand it. Remove any wedge of confusion that has created misunderstanding or miscommunication. Where there is behavior that needs to change in either of us, I pray You would enable that change to happen. As much as I try to hang on to my anger towards him because I feel it is justified. I want to do what You want Lord. I release all these feelings to You. Give me a renewed sense of love for my husband and words to heal this situation, this marriage.

I pray these things with all my heart. In Jesus' name. Amen

What "saved" me was the peace of God that covered me in all of my coming and going. He gave me restful sleep. When I would wake up and realize that "promised" call never happened, instead of worrying or becoming angry, God put peace in my heart. I would awaken to sweet songs playing and these same songs would carry me back to sleep.

I learned the peace of looking *up* versus looking *at* my mess. Trust in God with ALL your heart, as the scripture says. There is no room to doubt God when you trust Him. All things will be revealed in their due time…. But if it is never revealed, I had to ask myself if I would still trust in God? If God says "No" when I wanted Him to say "Yes", would I still trust Him? I started thinking of it like this, God is the One on the other side leading me to Him – through paths I cannot see. My light is dim without Him. Even walking with my arms straight in front of me, I cannot see the drop off… but God can! He will not let me fall. In fact, He is there to catch me if I do. So, I had to trust Him about everything above all else.

I've lost my smile
To the man I love
He carries it with him
Across the miles as he travels
He often wears it just for show
My smile is gone
While he is away
No glow about me
Just living day by day
Tears frequent my eyes

With thoughts of him
Prayers on my lips
To keep him covered
Till he is back with me again
Then I'll smile forever more…

Looking in the Rearview Mirror

Often when we are waiting or asking God to "fix" or "change: someone, He will focus on us. This has made me change my response, as I know I need work. I found when I did not know what to do, I prayed.

Romans 8:25-27 says, "But if we hope for what we do not see, we eagerly wait for *it* with perseverance. Likewise the Spirit also helps in our weaknesses. For we do not know what we should pray for as we ought, but the Spirit, Himself makes intercession for us with groanings which cannot be uttered. Now He who searches the heart knows what the mind of the Spirit is, because He makes intercession for the saints according to the *will* of God."

God's Word also says God knows what is in the heart so my prayers were not a surprise to God. It was just me admitting my weaknesses, my cry for help. I was faced with the true reality of my situation. Funny, is others may have seen the true picture but I was blinded to it and it was just becoming "real" to me.

In my desperation, I cried out to God. I knew He would hear me. I did not know what else to do but give God my cares and worries and fears. I had to come face-to-face with my assumptions and false beliefs so God could work on me and in me. I had to change my perspective.

Further, faith in God does not disappoint. A heart turned towards God will always have a good outcome. The challenge is turning from the things of the world and trusting in the unseen knowing and believing God is a good God who cares about everything that concerns us. I learned that God is truly always with me. He did not leave me. I left God. His love was still there waiting on me to run into His arms…which I gladly did, as I had no other place to go.

See although my heart yearned for my "husband", God knew I needed Him even more. Sometimes, you have to get to a place where you realize you cannot do anything on your own. A place where you recognize you are helpless without God. A place where you admit you cannot survive if God does not intervene. And it is there you will find God waiting for you with open arms.

Read: Psalm 40:1, Hebrews 10:22-25 & 11:1-3 and 1John 1:9

A Look in the Mirror   Date:

1. God wants ALL of you. How have you cried out to
   Him about your pain?

   _____
   _____
   _____
   _____
   _____
   _____

2. What has happened when you took your eyes off God
   and focused solely on your situation?

   _____
   _____
   _____
   _____
   _____
   _____

3. Have you ever prayed for God to "fix" the other
   person and God turned the mirror back to you?

   _____
   _____
   _____
   _____
   _____
   _____

God's Word:

"Now in the fourth watch of the night Jesus went to them, walking on the sea. And when the disciples saw Him walking on the sear, they were troubled, saying, 'It is a ghost!' And they cried out for fear. But immediately Jesus spoke to them, saying, 'Be of good cheer! It is I; do not be afraid.' And Peter answered Him and said, "Lord, if it is You, command me to come to You on the water.' So He said, 'Come.' And when Peter had come down out of the boat, he walked on the water to Jesus. But when he saw the wind was boisterous, he was afraid; and beginning to sink he cried out, saying, 'Lord, save me!' And immediately Jesus stretched out His hand and caught him, and said to him, 'O you of little faith, why did you doubt?' And when they got into the boat, the wind ceased." ~ Matthew 14:25-32

Prayer:

Lord, help me to keep my eyes on You in the midst of every storm. Increase my faith so I can walk on water and not be moved by the wind. Crush my fear and replace it with a solid faith in You. Lord, I confess I am often more afraid of what I see. Help me to trust more in the unseen and in Your hand so while I can't see with my physical eyes, I can see Your work. Further, Lord, help me to do all that You command me and to not turn from Your commands. In Jesus' Name, I pray. Amen.

Notes:

_____

_____

_____

_____

_____

_____

_____

_____

_____

_____

_____

_____

_____

_____

_____

_____

_____

_____

_____

_____

_____

_____

_____

_____

_____

_____

_____

_____

_____

_____

_____

Love Don't Live Here Anymore

IF I THOUGHT

If I thought love would hurt
I would have never breathed
If I thought my feelings would ever explode
I would have kept silent

If I thought I would become so overwhelmed
I would have continued to cry myself to sleep

But now my clear skies have shattered images
My thoughts unrelated
My voice unfamiliar

Oh, how I long to be free again
To think, without thinking
To love, without hurting
Feel without knowing
Scream without crying

And, oh yes, know who you are again.

A year after the move and my husband still had not moved. I continued to receive empty promises and I no longer believed he was moving. Two months before our second anniversary, the truth was fully revealed. He sent two-dozen roses to my job promising to see me that weekend, my birthday. He gave me some story about riding with a friend to Mexico first and then coming up to me afterwards. Well, the weekend came and went and I had not heard a word from him. I couldn't reach him by phone as the calls went straight to voicemail. I left several messages asking him to call and telling him I was worried and would call the police soon if I did not hear from him. Believe it or not, this was actually the first time he had committed to coming to visit and I could not reach him for days.

I did all I could until I finally felt the need to open a missing person's report. I thought something tragic must have happened. I recall having a pastor at my church pray for him. As she was praying, she told me, "He doesn't want to be found." I could not believe it! I didn't want to believe it. How could he not want to be found?? I was moved to do another background check. I had run a background check before we married but nothing came back. This one I did myself and the report came back with possible relatives. I had never met his mother or any other family since he told me they were estranged and that he hadn't had contact as he claimed to not "deal" with them because of how they treated him. I had never met his children because he always wanted it to be the "right time", although it never was right time. I thought his mother would still want to know her son was missing, regardless of their relationship. So, I sent letters to all the "possible relatives" on the reports asking them to call me.

When I found a number that I thought could be his mothers' I called to deliver this difficult news. I began sharing with her that I was his wife and that he was missing. She delivered a shock of her own. She said, "Honey, he is ALREADY married!" I was so confused. Maybe I had the wrong person. She told me he had been married for five years! I was appalled. I did not know how to respond. After answering her questions, she agreed to share my number with his "wife".

I never thought I would like the other woman, if there ever was one. But when I found out the "other woman" was actually my husband's first wife and that they were still married, the term "other woman" really referred to me. We talked the first night for nearly three hours piecing together the last three years I had spent with "our" husband. It was a moment of shock and disbelief, yet knowing the truth was really a kind of freedom. And through it all, I was overcome with peace. I did not feel alone – I felt the comfort of God. I felt a strong awareness of God's presence. It was one of the most unimaginable situations to be in and yet this was my life. This was her life.

Not sure why I was so surprised. He did cheat on me not more than three months after the engagement or at least that is when I found out. Of course, he was never faithful to me, only I did not know the full extent of his infidelities. When I confronted him in the past, he would apologize and give me some sob story about his weaknesses and how he was trying to overcome them. He would promise to be faithful going forward. He even told me all of his cheating days were BEFORE the wedding and so I forgave him.

Couldn't he have just told me then he was married and he couldn't go through with this?? Why did he leave that door open? That one piece of knowledge could have allowed me to close the door forever and given me the strength to move on. Sure, I would have been hurt and angry but I would have respected the truth, right? I found that just as with me, he left her with little explanation. But could it really be explained? He came back and we both allowed it. And that was my frustration not hers.

Over the next few days we would spend hours comparing stories and piecing together the holes in our lives. She ended our first conversation with, "I wish I could say it was nice talking to you… but under the circumstances…" I understood. I shared with her the information on the background check and the next day she called to tell me she found where he was living but he wasn't there. We suspected he was living with another woman. All I could think of was how this was continually getting worse.

As the reality of the situation hit me, I was filled with peace. I praised God continually for a "way out" of my marriage, as that is the way I viewed this new situation. If he was already married, my marriage did not exist. I don't know when the Spirit of God began to speak through me during our wife-to-wife conversations but He did and our conversations became more encouraging and focused on God. In our search for understanding, we both found God. It was a not so subtle reminder that God was in control. Over the next couple of months, we would pray together, cry together – all the while agreeing we met for this reason – to encourage one another in the things of God during this season. The season would end months later and we would part ways to deal with the situation on our own.

About five days or so into our meeting, I received a call from the police department that was yet another blow. The officer told me my "husband" had just returned into the country with "his wife". So, now there were three of us!!!! As hard as it was to digest the first wife, the third should not have been a surprise. We found out that he had traveled to South Africa with her to get married with her family present. I allowed and encouraged the first wife to talk to him first and try to understand the madness. I felt he really owed her an explanation. And since he was stopped at customs, he knew I knew about at least the third wife. In all honesty, I saw the reconciliation between him and his first wife as my exit strategy.

People may ask, "How would a loving God allow this to happen?" God's love is shown to us in many ways. First is in the allowance for us to make our own decisions. It was my decision - it was not based on God's will. Second, God revealed the truth to me – once I sought Him with all my heart and when He knew I was ready. I am hopeful in thinking I would have handled this "truth" better before the marriage but not fully sure if that would have been the case. Have you ever been in a situation where even if someone told you the truth – you would not believe it? Or worst, the truth would tear you apart? Don't get me wrong, the "truth" was not easy to hear or see but my strength was renewed! This was one of those times I have looked back and could clearly see it was not my strength that got me through. God, alone, carried me through this.

Thus, even as I planned a trip to confront him and meet wife number one and number three, I rejoiced. I believed God had worked a way for me out of this marriage without having to go through a divorce or a dishonoring of my vows. I was ecstatic! God had once again come to my rescue. He delivered me from a difficult, traumatic situation proving His faithfulness once again, in spite of me. I thought this awful ordeal was finally over. Little did I know that God still had more for me to learn before He would fully release me from this marriage.

Looking in the Rearview Mirror

You really have to believe and know that what is a "surprise" to us, is not a surprise to God. God is all knowing. And often He will open our eyes if we are willing to truly see. Deception is a type of blindness. Once in a web of deception, we are blinded to the truth. God's Word says, "The Lord opens the eyes of the blind. The Lord lifts up those who are weighted down. The Lord loves the godly (Psalm 146:8 NLT).

Reality, my "husband" was a good liar. He played the deception game well. He knew my weaknesses and used them against me. He used my strengths against me also. He had me convinced he was involved in illegal dealings and that he kept details from me to "protect me". I did not know any details only it was something of which I would not approve. Thus, I suspected it was dangerous. I knew it included lots of travel – driving long distances… or so he told me. So, we always talked that if he were ever unreachable for an extended amount of time, I would put out a missing person's report.

I also truly believed something happened in Mexico. I rationalized there were many legitimate reasons I had not heard from him… yet, thinking he was already married and had left the country to marry again, had *never* crossed my mind. He did just enough of keeping his word on some things that I did not question everything.

Yet, when faced with the reality of the situation, I was still relieved that everything was out in the light. I had all the facts and I could deal with it. Truly, I thought this was my way out, which I was more concerned with then anything else. I felt God had heard my cries of "I'm sorry!" and He was using this situation to release me from my situation.

The interesting thing is you are able to operate one way when you are in the dark and that same behavior is not acceptable once truth has been revealed. It is one thing to *think* something is wrong and quite another to *know* what is wrong. Knowing requires action. It requires change. And most of the time, it requires God.

Read: 2 Samuel 2:6, John 8:32, and Psalm 25:4-6

A Look in the Mirror   **Date:**

1. How has God answered your prayers in the dark times?

   _____

   _____

   _____

   _____

   _____

   _____

   _____

2. What has been worse: the pain of knowing or the pain of not knowing? How have you handled both knowing and/or not knowing?

   _____

   _____

   _____

   _____

   _____

   _____

   _____

3. What has been your response when God has revealed truth to you?

   _____

   _____

   _____

   _____

   _____

   _____

   _____

God's Word:

"Thus my heart was grieved, and I was vexed in my mind. I was so foolish and ignorant; I was like a beast before You. Nevertheless I am continually with You; You hold me by my right hand. You will guide me with Your counsel, and afterward receive me to glory. Whom have I in heaven but You? And there is none upon earth that I desire besides You. My flesh and my heart fail; But God is the strength of my heart and my portion forever. For indeed, those who are far from You shall perish; You have destroyed all those who desert You for harlotry. But it is not good for me to draw near to God; I have put my trust in the Lord God; I have put my trust in the Lord GOD, that I may declare all Your works." ~ Psalm 73:21-28

Prayer:

Lord, I thank You that You are always near and that You always have me. Even when I make bad choices or decisions, You are there. I thank You for Your truth that illuminates the darkness. I thank You for Your strength when I am weak. Help me to remember You are all I need. Draw me nearer to You and help me to trust in You more. May I continually declare Your works even when I don't see Your hand, as I know Your heart. In Jesus' Name, I pray. Amen.

Notes:

_____

_____

_____

_____

_____

_____

_____

_____

_____

_____

_____

_____

_____

_____

_____

_____

_____

_____

_____

_____

_____

_____

_____

_____

_____

_____

_____

_____

_____

_____

_____

_____

Can I Forget It Ever Happened?

All of it?
The pain, the heartache – even the feelings of love that
lead down that path
I say "down" as no matter how "high" I felt,
It was always "down"
Is there a place past denial, past resentment, past
avoidance
Where I can truly forget it ever happened?
Truly ALL of it.
The me, the you, the us.
The parts where I looked into
Your eyes and was lost
In what I liked to call
My fantasyland
The reality is where I now live
Without you
So, can we turn it around –
Let the fantasy be your existence?
What is really lost with memories
Of you and us?
I mean - there is still –
A me – right?
Has to be – because
I'm still here and you're not
So, let's forget it ever happened
The love, the laughs, the hugs, the kisses, the private
moments
Because all of the "happiness" was buried anyway
And replaced with grief
Abuse - emotionally, physically, psychologically ---
And even spiritually… How did I let it happen?
Did I transform you into my God?

Did I begin to worship you, rather than my God?
Did I put you before my God?
The answer is simply Yes.
Reality check….
You Are NOT my GOD!!!
My God is faithful.
He loves unconditionally.
He protects.
He provides.
He is consistent…
The same yesterday, today, and tomorrow.
My God never lies – His Word is true.
I've noticed something…
The more I look UP to my God,
The less I see of you.

Where Do I Go From Here?

I had many regrets especially when it comes to my ex-husband. Surely, had I known he had so many secrets and lies of that magnitude I would have changed all of my future actions. After all, I prayed many times; was what I continually reminded myself. I loved the Lord but I was not obedient to Him or His Word. I sought the Lord in many of my steps but I did not wait on the Lord. I don't know why my heart opened up to that man the way it did. I tried to do things differently. My love was real. My intentions were real.

A TWINKLE

I saw a star twinkle
I thought it was for me
I poured my energies into
This love I thought was real

I thought this was the answer to my prayers, my
loneliness
And most importantly, my pain
I was happy, although scared
Scared to believe it was the real thing

But as my faith became stronger
My lovely picture began to fade
I tried to hold on to it
Pray harder, but still it faded

And as it begins to disappear
I realize with tears in my eyes
And pain in my heart

That twinkle was not meant for me

I prayed with all sincerity for God's will for the possibility of a relationship and marriage. So, why did it continue? God could have slammed the door in my face. Was it my free will being exercised? Was God testing my heart for Him? I am sure He was. Was it a plot of the devil to ruin the plans God had for me? I can't fully blame the devil either. I made choices. I prayed but did not listen. I only prayed for my way. I allowed this man to stay in my life after he continued to show me he did not want to stay. Even with all this, I knew God had a purpose for my trial.

I know the promise of Romans 8:28, which says, "And we know that in all things God works for the good of those who love Him, who have been called according to His purpose." And no matter the plan or the purpose, God used the situation to draw me closer to Him. Where I was not listening before or only wanted to hear the answers pleasing to me, I now sought what was pleasing to God.

"Okay, Lord, I trust You. But can you tell me how this will end?" Funny thing is I know the "but" in my question just contradicts my statement and so did God. He said, "Do you trust Me?" I said, "Yes, I trust You". God said, "If you trust Me then it doesn't matter how it ends?" That is really the whole point. Trusting God is having faith in the things unseen. Trusting God is not like trusting man. God doesn't lie. God is faithful.

Hebrews 11:1 states, *"Now faith is being sure* (substance) *of what we hope for and certain* (evidence) *of what we do not see"*. Romans 8:24-25 states, *"But hope that is seen is no hope at all. Who hopes for what he already has? But if we hope for what we do not have, we wait patiently for it"*.

Patience is not my strongest virtue. Patience is built through trials. The key is often that we go "THROUGH" trials. We do not stay there. I learned that if we stop complaining and whining about them, we may actually see God receive the glory from our faith. God knows the beginning and the end. God knows every little detail – even those details we often overlook. And God loves us beyond measure. If only we can fully understand the depth of God's love... we will see all that we go through so differently. So, I had to rest in Him and cast all my cares upon Him. I had to stay in the moment and trust that God was in full control. So again, I prayed... more like cried my heart out to God daily.

Dear Lord,
I am on my way to put some reality to this current life of mine. I pray for Your protection. I praise You, Lord, for the things that have been brought to light. I thank You for the strength You've given me as well as the comfort. I don't know if I am doing the right thing. I only know that I trust You. I trust You whatever the outcome. May You receive the Glory. Holy Spirit, please direct my thoughts and actions and words. Please be with all of us through this ordeal. I love you, Lord. I praise Your name, Jesus. Amen.

Thank You, Heavenly Father, for covering my travels. Thank You for allowing me to hear You. You are a gracious God. I love You and I still trust You for whatever the outcome of this whole situation. Today, Lord, I am overcome with the lies. I feel pain over these lies my "husband" has told and continues to tell. I hurt Lord... I must confess I am hurt and upset. My "husband" is treating me as if I did something wrong. I

was a faithful wife. A little rebellious at times, but I tried
to please You, Lord. I feel like crap. I feel unworthy. I
feel like I committed adultery – like I should have
known. I pray for Your guidance and direction, yet I
know I must fully submit to You Lord and allow You to
intercede on my behalf. I must trust You and above all, I
must have faith. Lord, I confess, when I talk to his first
wife, I feel less than, like an intruder in her life. I hurt.
My "husband" was never a real/true husband to me. I
feel so cheated. Why did I have to endure all of this?
Was it to bring me to this time? Please speak to me,
Lord, and open my ears to hear. Thank You, Dear God.
Amen.

Dear Heavenly Father,
Please forgive me for trying to move ahead of You.
Forgive me for wanting this test; this trial to be over
before You have said it is over. Forgive me for doubting
You and not fully trusting You to handle this situation. I
am having a hard time with this. I want to cry Lord, so
badly. I want to be released from this pain. I want to
know the outcome – why won't he let me go? Lord, what
is your plan for me. I know I should trust You whatever
the outcome and I do... I just want a peek into the
outcome. Something to put my heart to rest. Something
from You before I hear from anyone else. Lord, can you
give me a glimpse of this outcome – please? And if it is
not Your will for me to know, can You help me be patient
till You are ready for me to know? Strengthen my faith in
You. Give me a faith that cannot be shaken. I need Your
guidance. I need Your reassurance. I am dependent on
You Lord, to tell me, move me, direct me, pick me up and
turn me around if need be. Do what you have to do to get
me through this still standing. Break me so I may be
rebuilt by You. Amen.

I really thought seeing the other wives would make the situation easier to handle. I thought confronting my "husband" would help to put closure to the whole mess. I even, wrongly, thought God would let me out of my marriage immediately. I was so very wrong. Things just seemed to stand still while progressively becoming worst, if that was possible.

The 1st wife had a combative nature and it appeared their marriage was plagued by many of these loud arguments and fights. I was not accustomed to that, but it explained a lot. The 3rd wife was complacent and not realistic. She determined she would "fight" for her marriage. I could not understand her. If I didn't have a marriage, she surely didn't. She was the older of us three. She was fighting for her pride. She had taken this man to her country and married him in the presence of her family. Surely she could not reveal to her family that he had two other wives. Honestly, I just wanted out. I really thought it would be that easy. But God had more work to do in me.

I realized I needed some type of connection to keep reality in my situation. I kept in contact with his mom and the first wife and I would talk occasionally, which was a very unnatural relationship. Selfishly, we both had our own needs and reasons to keep in contact. Our "husband" was still living with the 3rd wife, while trying to convince both of us that it wasn't his will to be there. I did not maintain contact with the 3rd wife. Honestly, I was bothered that he chose to stay with her and not me or the 1st wife. I was mad that he was living with her but never "lived" with me.

I prayed for all three of them. I was constantly looking for my way out while trying to understand what the Lord wanted me to do and wanting to not feel anything.

Father, I'm struggling. I can't hear Your voice. What have I done? Are my motives wrong? They are. I know I cannot do things for selfish gain. Forgive me, Father. I feel so lost. I so want to be free of all of this. Forgive me for trying to continually take this away from You. I feel rejected. I am angry. I feel stupid that I got into this situation. I am fighting not to regret the whole thing. I want to accept this marriage as over...this marriage that never was. I wanted the wrong things. I wanted to be married. I thought through my prayers that he was the one. How can this be explained, Lord? How can I redeem myself? Why do I still love him? Why can't I let go? Is it my fear that I will be unable to marry again? Is it my fear of having to trust and love another man, so I stick to the broken one I know? Is it my past that keeps constantly repeating itself? I feel so much pain, Lord. I want to release the pain. I don't want to hurt anymore. I am thankful for this trial in my life. I am thankful for the growth... yet I know it is only the beginning. I am thankful for the truth. I only want this to be resolved. I don't feel comfortable being married to a man who has two other wives. He doesn't even know who he is. Funny... I don't know who I am....

Lord, I felt the need to watch the video of our unlawful marriage looking for telltale signs that my "husband" knew what he was doing was wrong. Unlike with the 3rd wife, he had plenty of time to get out of marrying me. Why, Lord, did he come back? Why did he still do this? How could he lie before You, God, and pretend he did not have another wife? I doubt the whole existence of my marriage. There were too many things too good to be true. *My wants and desires overshadowed everything bad about him. Was I just willing to settle? Did I feel I went too far to turn back? Did I just not trust in You, Lord? Yes, Lord, I have many regrets. Tell me where do I go from here? How do I recover from this? Does this situation have a happy ending? And if so, for whom? What is my next step? I can't stay in this place forever. Lord, help me to know Your will. Help me to know what direction to go, what path to walk. I don't want to do anything else to disappoint You, Lord. I just want to get through this and prove that You, Lord, can be trusted in the midst of difficult times and that through these times, You are truly all we need. I want my faith to shine through so there is no doubt in anyone's eyes that I worship You. Thank You. Amen.*

Looking in the Rearview Mirror

Psalm 28:1-2 (New Living Translation) says, "I pray to you, O Lord, my rock. Do not turn a deaf ear to me. For if You are silent, I might as well give up and die. Listen to my prayer for mercy as I cry out to You for help, as I lift my hands towards Your Holy sanctuary."

The prayers I shared are real and unedited, maybe condensed in some cases, but real all the same. The struggle was real. I was caught up in the veracity of my decisions, my choices. I have found that sharing my heart with God opens me up to hear from Him.

I believe we know God has the answers – the question is always do we want His "answers" or our own way. Impatience gets in the way. I wanted things in my time. I was torn. I wanted to trust God but I also wanted things to work out to my benefit – whatever I thought that would be.

We often forget God does not need our help in any situation. He wants our fully submitted heart to Him. We have to get to a place where we repent quickly and give the situation to God and leave it there. Trust Him for the outcome. Yes, we will do things we regret and pray we can do over but even in those regrets, hopefully there is learning.

Hopefully we will have gained knowledge and insight that will keep us from falling into the exact trap again and help others who may fall. I was guilty of thinking God needed my assistance. I thought God needed to know I was being faithful and that I did not feel I deserved this type of "marriage". Yet, all God wanted was my heart.

Trusting in God is action even when we are standing still in the midst of chaos. We have to get to a place where the storm doesn't move us because we know God is faithful and is there to catch us when we fall.

1 Corinthians 10:13 (The Message version) says, "No test or **temptation** that comes your way is beyond the course of what others have had to face. All you need to remember is that God will never let you down; he'll never let you be pushed past your limit; he'll always be there to help you come through it." This is hard to remember when we are in the trench of tragedy and feel the waves are about to overtake us. Which is why we often have to encourage ourselves and remind ourselves of God's promises.

Read: 2 Samuel 22:7, Psalm 57:1-3, and Mark 14:38

A Look in the Mirror   **Date:**

1. What has been your response when God did not answer your prayer?

   _____

   _____

   _____

   _____

   _____

   _____

   _____

2. What regrets do you have over decisions you've made?

   _____

   _____

   _____

   _____

   _____

   _____

   _____

3. What advice would you give to a friend in a relationship such as this?

   _____

   _____

   _____

   _____

   _____

   _____

   _____

God's Word:

"Consider it pure joy, my brothers and sisters, whenever you face trials of many kinds, because you know that the testing of your faith produces perseverance. Let perseverance finish its work so that you may be mature and complete, not lacking anything. If any of you lacks wisdom, you should ask God, who gives generously to all without finding fault, and it will be given to you. But when you ask, you must believe and not doubt, because one who doubts is like a wave of the sea, blown and tossed by the wind. That person should not expect to receive anything from the Lord. Such a person is double-minded and unstable in all they do. ~ James 1:2-8

Prayer:

Father, forgive me for the times I have despised trials. I don't always consider my trials that of joy. I am slowly finding that my trials strengthen my faith and help me to persevere. So, I thank you for my trials, as without them, I would not know the flaws or weak spots in my faith. I thank you for bestowing wisdom just by my asking. Your wisdom helps me to maneuver in the difficult times in my life. Father, I ask You with all faith to give me wisdom in my daily walk. Help me to make the right decisions and to know the way I should go. Thank You for always going before me and for holding me through each trail I encounter. I know You are always with me and will never leave me. In Jesus' Name, I pray. Amen.

Notes:

_____

_____

_____

_____

_____

_____

_____

_____

_____

_____

_____

_____

_____

_____

_____

_____

_____

_____

_____

_____

_____

_____

_____

_____

_____

_____

_____

_____

_____

_____

_____

_____

Really God, Really?!?!

"But I tell you who hear me: Love your enemies, do good to those who hate you, bless those who curse you, pray for those who mistreat you. If someone strikes you on one cheek, turn to him the other also. If someone takes your cloak, do not stop him from taking your tunic. Give to everyone who asks you, do not demand it back. Do to others as you would have them do to you." Luke 6: 27 – 31.

And the Lord said to me, "Pray for him!" I couldn't believe the Lord was asking me to pray for that man. I said, "Really, God! Really!!! You want me to pray for him!" Hadn't I prayed for him enough when we were "married"? Unbelievable! I wanted an annulment – a "void" of my marriage. I wanted it as though he – we NEVER happened!! How awesome would that be?? I'm thinking this was how I have lived my life all along, erasing things from my memory, but if I pray for him – it's as though he still exists – right? Does that mean I can't go on like he never happened?

One condition of my answered prayer was for me to pray for my ex. In the midst of all this – I felt caught. Why me? Isn't there someone else left to pray for him? For goodness sake, he had two other wives! Couldn't one of them pray for him? Or his mother? Yes, that was me trying to rationalize with God! Now, that was funny! I can definitely relate to the purpose of praying for your enemies but I did not want anything to do with my ex, including prayer. To be obedient, I would pray, "Bless him, Lord" and hoped that satisfied my commitment.

God told me to pray for my ex – it was a struggle. It took a couple of years with me providing insincere sounding prayers thinking it would please God – but that was only partial obedience – if you could even call it that. I had to get to the point where I prayed for him as I would a close family relative, like my child. I felt I had already poured enough of my energies praying for that man, I just didn't want to pray for him anymore. I didn't think he deserved any blessing or covering, as I would pray for my son. I did not want to have to speak his name in prayer. I didn't want to think of him. I felt I had done my part. So why was God requiring more of me.

I pray for you because I know I need to
You have hurt many others and me, but still…
I must pray for you to keep me from turning from you
and
I must pray for you, as I realize, praying for you is God's will
Yet, I must pray with forgiveness in my heart of any wrong you have done
God says I must forgive others as HE forgives me
Therefore, I pray for you and the destructive path I see you on
Even as I am blind to my own destruction
Through faith, I acknowledge only God knows what is in our hearts
Moreover, with my heart I must pray for you

I slowly figured out my unwillingness to pray for him was a reflection of my heart not being right. I was still holding on to unforgiveness and bitterness. See I was okay in praying for my ex when I thought it would help him do the right thing. For me, "doing the right thing," meant being with one wife and releasing the rest of us from the bond. He could not do that. He was used to manipulating a situation and people. And truth be told, I felt I had prayed enough prayers for him that I should not be given that mandate from God. Yes, I thought I deserved not to be held to that command. I was wrong.

It took me a long time to realize that by praying for my ex – I was actually benefitting me – it was not for him. It took time for me to release and then forgive. I had to get to a place where I knew I was disobeying God by not praying for him or forgiving him and that was sinning. Then I had to act. God's request of me did not change – it was always there. Funny thing is God did not leave me during my period of rebellion, which lasted over a few years. I came to realize that my act of disobedience was a barrier to my breakthrough. I have since learned that when I minister to others I encourage myself. There is a level of trust that must be reached where we whole-heartedly believe God can handle everything and everyone better than we can… thus we release them into His capable hands.

I pray for your protection – coming and going
For your discernment and sensitivity to God's Word
I pray for God to guide you in every step that you take
That you will find shelter in HIS Word and under HIS
wing
And through my praying for you… I pray for me
For my protection, my discernment, and my sensitivity
to God's Word
I pray for you that I may find God to lead my way and
guide my steps
I pray for my shelter under HIS wings

It is just a generous gift we give to others who have hurt us when we pray for them; we are also allowing God to work in us. We pray for their health, their protection, their relationship with God, and even their prosperity. That prayer is a release for us to allow God to have His perfect will. We don't pray to say we have "approved" of a person's behavior but we do need to accept the person as "worthy" of God's love and provision. This is where we remember - none of us are perfect – not one. I reminded myself that God sacrificed His only begotten Son for my sins thus the least I could do was pray for that man. And the Lord knew that man needed prayer.

Forgiveness is not a once and done. We often have to forgive the same offense over and over again. What encourages me is God forgives me – continually. I know He may have often thought I was not the brightest bulb on the tree as I often got myself into messes that could have been avoided. Unforgiveness is like passing judgment and the scripture says, "Judge not, lest you be judged" or the one that says, "With the same measure you judge others, you will be judged" (Matt 7:2). When we hold an offense against others, we are judging their deed and believe that they are not worthy of forgiveness.

It's a process – forgiveness, grief, all of it. We have to trust God with the little and big things. He is faithful, able, and worthy. I wanted to be used as a vessel to help others but I was struggling myself. I had trouble completely forgiving. It was definitely a daily walk. Things I had not thought about in a while that he did or said would come into my head and I had to deal with each event. It was not a blanket "I forgive him" type of thing. It was more of I forgive him for this, and for this, and for this, and for this, etc. I guess that is why God says you have to forgive multiple times.

Many times when we go through a bad ordeal we often just want to forget about it. Not re-live it. Not even admit it happened. After being in a painful relationship, I felt the same with my marriage. So imagine my disappointment when God did not immediately let me out. I so wanted the first wife to keep him. I even told her this might just be God's plan for her. Then she asked me, "What if God tells you to stay with him?" I was sickened at the thought. Surely He revealed the truth of this cheater for me to have a way out without any fault of my own. I was faced with wanting to be obedient to the Lord and wanting to walk away.

The challenge is to forgive those who wish you harm and pray for them. Have faith that God will take care of the rest. Sure, we have risks in loving – if you are only looking at the flesh side of things. But spiritually, what do you have to lose??? God commands us to love. He will deal with those who harm us but we must be responsible to God first and then to ourselves.

Sometimes you just have to say it is in the past and I am walking into the future God has for me. If not, you will leave the door open to other areas that you have not addressed. I have to say the hardest thing in my "marriage" was treating my husband like a husband, especially when I didn't feel he was acting like one (to me anyway). It was difficult to treat him like the man I felt he should be when he behaved so differently. I had difficulty loving him in spite of all his flaws. Even more, was forgiving him after I learned the truth.

There were many times I asked God, "Do you see what he is doing? He is not honoring you." God quickly corrected me by stating to me to focus on Him and be obedient to Him and He will deal with my husband. But, as long as I was looking at my husband

and pointing at his wrong doings, I was not focused on God and what I should be doing.

One incident in particular was when my husband lied to me about some money he received. I believed him and was ready to take down the whole bank to find my money. In the course of this, the bank showed me that the money went back to my husband. The absence of this money caused the house I was selling to go delinquent with this payment now missing. And there was no way to replace that money.

I was so enraged! So angry that all I saw was red – fire. I couldn't even drive home I was so upset. I remember walking around a store in a daze. I bought a desk and proceeded home to put it together. In the time between the bank, the store, and home – I called my husband a few times and left some real enraged messages on his voicemail. He knew I went to the bank and I knew he was not answering purposely. What I later found out was he used that money to help his first wife pay on the new house she was buying – like he was contributing. I am not sure how I would have responded had I known the truth back then!

Through the process of putting together my desk, the Lord began to deal with me. "Look at you! You are behaving just like him! You are so angry over material things! You've allowed his actions to cause you to sin!"

I was so disgusted with myself. I could not believe I reacted that way. All the time I was trying to convince God how awful he was and I was no better. Has that ever happened to you? Have you ever been so wrapped up in another person's sin that they seemed to get away with, that you lost your own way and sinned? I was faced with my own judgment.

I found it is much easier, at times, to forgive when the person is not around and completely out of your life than it is when the person is around. Every time I thought I had forgiven him, he would contact me and I would have to start the process all over again. I dreaded when someone would ask about him because soon I would hear from him. I called him the devil because every time I thought I was rid of him, he reappeared. I blocked his email address, changed my phone number, yet somehow he still found a way to contact me. I was challenged with not being able to forget and still forgive, as the pain and anger would arise with each contact.

It took me a long time to get to a place where I wanted to forgive and realized I could not do it alone. The pain ran too deep. There was so much hurt and so many lies. How could I just forgive him? I wanted to erase him from my memory and have that count for something. I felt if I could do that then I would not have the thoughts of unforgiveness. I could consider him forgotten, thus not having a need to forgive.

But my logic was flawed. The bible, unfortunately, does not provide a way out of not forgiving a person. There is not a scripture that reads, "If a person lies and cheats on you, you don't have to forgive the person." Or "If you are unable to completely forget the incident or the person, you are not held to forgive." What I failed to learn at the time is forgiveness is for the person who was offended not the person who caused the offense.

As long as I held on to the bitterness, anger and even hurt, I was the one struggling. I was the one consumed. I was the one holding on to him in my emotions, albeit negative emotions. I was the one stuck. He was free to continue to lie and live his life. Forgiveness is releasing the person from your hold and giving them to God for His handling of them. Problem is you cannot tell God what to do with the person. You have to trust God to handle the person the way He chooses. You have to release the person from your judgment and how you feel they should be punished. When you are free from the emotional bondage holding you to a person, free through forgiving the person, you are also free to move on. You are ready for the healing process to begin.

Looking in the Rearview Mirror

Plain and simple, forgiveness is a choice.... a willful choice and not an easy choice when you are hurting. I honestly struggled with forgiving my ex. I wanted to just forget and move on. Bury the pain and the past. But God would not allow me to do so out of His love for me. He loved me enough to not allow me to stay were I was and how I was. Yet, I fought it. I tried to reason with God. I tried to plead my case as to why someone other than me should be the one to pray.

The more I rebelled against God, the more upset I was with God for requesting something like that of me. Surely, God knew what I had just been through which was probably His reasons for telling me to pray for him. I truly did not want to pray for him. I wanted the situation over and done and buried.

Truth is we often want to see the people who hurt us suffer. It takes a great deal of faith to want to see the person saved. I didn't want this man blessed without being convicted in his actions. I was suffering. I was in pain. Shouldn't he at least be bothered? I felt if he truly "loved" me, he should feel horrible pain by how he treated me and those feelings should keep him up at night.

The flaw in my thinking was I wanted to play God and administer judgment, otherwise I couldn't truly forgive him. Yet, God told me to pray for him. Praying for him was for me. I needed to release the feelings. I needed to cut the tie, the bond. I needed to seek God for my healing and pray for this man. I knew if anyone could change him, God could. Once I was able to pray and release him to God, I was at peace. I did not need to know his fate. I needed to be obedient and release him.

And by doing so, God was able to do a work in me. I could forgive myself. I could move on. And that is one of the most important aspects of forgiveness… your forgiving releases the person and *you* from the incident and you move on.

Read: 1 Samuel 15:22, Psalm 130:35 and Hebrews 5:8

A Look in the Mirror   **Date:**

1. What bitterness are you still holding on to?

_____
_____
_____
_____
_____
_____
_____

2. Do you hold any unforgiveness in your heart against God?

_____
_____
_____
_____
_____
_____
_____

3. If the person you "forgave" wanted to come back into your life, how would you feel?

_____
_____
_____
_____
_____
_____
_____

God's Word:

"'For if you forgive men their trespasses, your heavenly Father will also forgive you. But if you do not forgive men their trespasses, neither will your Father forgive your trespasses.'" ~ Matthew 6:14-15

"Then Peter came to Him and said, 'Lord, how often shall my brother sin against me, and I forgive him? Up to seven times?' Jesus said to him, 'I do not say to you, up to seven times, but up to seventy times seven.'" ~ Matthew 18:21-22

Prayer:

Father, I confess it is often difficult to forgive at times, especially when I feel I have been wronged. Yet, Your Word says to the extent we forgive or don't forgive others will be the same measurement of forgiveness we will have ourselves. Lord, I ask You to help me to forgive those who have hurt me. Help me to forgive those who have lied and stolen from me. Help me to not hold any offense but to quickly release it all to You. I want to walk in forgiveness. I want Your blessings. I do not want to hold onto any bitterness or unforgiveness. I ask that You reveal to me any unforgiveness or bitterness within me and help me to release and bless those I have not released. I ask this prayer in the Name of Jesus. Amen.

Notes:

_____

_____

_____

_____

_____

_____

_____

_____

_____

_____

_____

_____

_____

_____

_____

_____

_____

_____

_____

_____

_____

_____

_____

_____

_____

_____

_____

_____

_____

Let the Healing Begin

Healing is a process. It takes time. I learned this valuable lesson when I had surgery to remove a cyst on my tailbone. When the cyst first appeared, I didn't know what it was. I only knew that there was pain in my back every time I sat down, especially when my back would rub against a chair. My doctor advised surgery to remove the cyst and prevent the reoccurrence of another cyst. So I believed once I had the surgery to remove the cyst I would be pain free. But that was not the case.

My incision did not heal properly. Every doctor visit, I would have to endure the re-opening of the incision area to encourage the wound to heal properly. It was pure torture… all over a small section that refused to close. The doctor would burn the skin, per se, to open the wound and hope the "natural" healing process would kick in. I endured several treatments of this before my wound finally healed.

I would love to say it was a quick process but it wasn't. Just like my trips to the doctor, the healing process was long and painful. I wasn't able to heal myself; I had to depend on the doctor to help me heal. Sad thing is the nurse was so sweet and the doctor was a true Christian, so I couldn't blame them for my lack of healing. The nurse felt my pain each time and just held my hand. They didn't enjoy inflicting pain upon me anymore than I did. They both knew what I didn't that if the wound were not re-opened, my condition would worsen.

This is very similar to the process we endure to heal our hearts. We think cutting off a relationship through separation or divorce can heal us of the pain but unfortunately it is not that easy. Many times healing takes work. It may take sacrifice. It may take an emptying out of the things that are keeping you ill. We can even *think* we are healed until we encounter an experience that shows us that our "wounds" are not completely gone. Our wounds may need to be re-opened by addressing past issues for the wound to heal properly. In all cases, we cannot heal on our own... we need God to help us in the healing process and we have to desire the healing.

A Man Healed at the Pool of Bethesda (John 5:2-9)
*Now there is in Jerusalem by the Sheep Gate a pool, which is called in Hebrew, Bethesda, having five porches. In these lay a great multitude of sick people, blind, lame, paralyzed, waiting for the moving of the water. For an angel went down at a certain time into the pool and stirred up the water; then whoever stepped in first, after the stirring of the water, was made well of whatever disease he had. Now a certain man was there who had an infirmity thirty-eight years. When Jesus saw him lying there, and knew that he already had been in that condition a long time, He said to him, "**Do you want to be made well?**"*

The sick man answered Him, "Sir, I have no man to put me into the pool when the water is stirred up; but while I am coming, another steps down before me."

Jesus said to him, "Rise, take up your bed and walk." And immediately the man was made well, took up his bed, and walked.

This scripture sat in my spirit for a long time. When I read it during my healing time, the Lord said this was directed at me. In my pause, I allowed examination of my life and found this was an appropriate question. I hope as I examine me, you also examine you. Although I don't have any illness, major or otherwise, I would often trivialize my own issues for the sake of those with more important or major issues. I would opt for others to go to the "pool" before me, as if God is not enough to heal us all. I minimized my needs and opt for God to help others more in need – thinking they are more important yet, God is still God and able to meet ALL needs and still have more left. I would opt to take meds for my headache or ignore my tooth pain, as if that will allow God to help someone with cancer or brain tumors. Surely, He can't be concerned with my small pain when there are people facing life and death situations.

Many times I found excuses why I couldn't come to God for my needs. This is not just physical healing but emotional as well. It's not that I didn't believe God could heal me – I just saw greater needs, so I didn't ask. Often we don't think or feel we are worthy of healing.

For years prior to my marriage, I refused to re-open a wound for healing. I thought by not thinking about it or forgetting about the situation would heal me. I was wrong. Healing often requires both exposing these wounds, hurts, disappointments, fears, etc. and releasing them. I learned that if you do not heal properly or if the natural healing does not occur, the wound remains open and susceptible to further injury.

I adverted healing. I had dark places I didn't want revealed. I may have even thought I was healed. Thus, healing required work on my part. To begin with, I had to have enough faith to believe that healing was possible. I would have to go through the pain of dealing with my wounds.

I had to come to terms with how my past wounds brought me to my current state. I did not feel I deserved love so I settled for anything. I thought fighting for love meant staying with a man who refused to commit and only wanted me on his terms. So I stayed when I should have left… many times. I always seemed to fall for someone who didn't feel the same and couldn't return the feelings. I didn't understand or know how to heal. I'd go out of my way to be accepted, loved, cherished, needed, cared for, appreciated, thought of and fulfilled versus being happy to just be and allow these things to come and go on their own. I punished myself by avoiding love. This is where I found myself after the void in my marriage. I punished myself for my sins. I felt I didn't deserve love from anyone. I was not even allowing God to love me.

NUMB

I've found a place where I am numb
Or maybe you found it
That point where I can't feel anymore…
I can't run.
I can't hide.
Have I been here before?
I can't tell for sure
Stick a needle in me
Do I bleed?
I can't tell for sure
I feel nothing
I have no clear thought or memory
I am numb.

One day, I found I had a new skill. Not just a skill, I found I was an expert. My new expertise was a mason, a wall builder. See years of pain, heartbreak, disappointment, betrayal… you name it, all this gave me the experience to build my skill. With each painful experience, I made cement blocks. I did not use dry wall, too weak. I built solid walls; brick by brick, until my heart was enclosed in its own safe place.

Do you know what walls do? They shut things and people out and keep people and things in. I found I was pretty good at building these walls. Nothing could get in…. but I also could not get out. Do you think this caused problems? See, the walls were meant to protect me from every kind of hurt I experienced: the absence of a father; the rejection of men and friends; and the disappointment and heartbreak of failed relationships. The pain from lies I bought into and every pain. I did not want to feel pain.

Problem is, I found I not only shut out pain, I shut out all feelings. My wall was so strong and impenetrable; nothing could get in or out. It didn't seem to bother me until I wanted to feel joy, love, happiness, and the good feelings. There is something about not being able to choose what feelings you want to let in and which you want to keep out. People do not come with signs on their forehead stating, "I am here to deceive you and I will cause you pain!" or "I come in peace." Thus, you take risks at whom to allow into your barricade. But God! God is perfect love. But to allow Him in, the walls I built around my heart had to come down.

A heart without walls… what an interesting concept! Without God, it is impossible. As daily, we are presented with things that force us to keep our guard up. Throughout life, we experience a host of trials and tribulations that make us add layers to our heart – as sort of protection. Breaking down walls entails making a decision to trust. Trust God first of all. When we trust

God, we trust Him with our heart and we trust Him in His entirety. Meaning, we trust the plans He has for us and His protection of us. We must trust God completely.

I have personally seen God remove people from my life and I have also seen when I have held on when He wanted me to let go. There is pain either way but I seem to have prolonged my pain when I tried to hold on to what I was meant to release. Sometime pain can be like a cut. It hurts when it happens but it heals. We can pick the scab off or re-injure ourselves or we can allow the natural process to heal us. With each hurt, we grow and develop. Our feeling reminds us we are alive. We are still part of the living. The absence of pain, is often just denial or the result of walls we have built to block our feelings.

It's the dreams that die unfulfilled that leave us the emptiest. A father / daughter relationship that fails due to an absent father and broken promises. The husband / wife who cannot seem to make it work. When love is not enough or until one in the party no longer exists. Is love really lost? Or just forgotten?

For the father who walked – built a new life, yet left the first family, broken and abused. When does the healing come? When is the parent strong enough to do the right thing?

I long for the healing of families and marriages. I still root for the success of both especially when there is a real fight to make it work. I long for when the bible – God's Word is no longer just "words" but the very foundation and framework that hold everything together and His Holy Spirit, His breath, and His blood which all speak life into all that has died.

True love should know no boundaries. True love should last amidst the strife and chaos because true love is of God. So let our hearts not be deceived into doing what's wrong; into believing what's not true – let truth be our guide.

When does the healing begin? When we allow healing to strengthen us to move beyond the pain and fear. When we allow God's Word to be the very blood that flows through our body – stronger than the air we breathe. Yet, we often see only words on a page – never allowing those words to penetrate our very being.

Life is full of hurts – all kinds – yet there is very little healing. We pick at the scabs to continue the pain or promote our scars to either justify our pain or limit us from healing.

Silent Sufferers of Pain

There are those of us who walk around with a smile
While our insides bleed in agony
We live lives of normalcy
While our brains throb constantly with trauma
There are those of us whose smile
Cannot hide the pain in our eyes
Whose hearts are one beat
From exploding into tiny pieces
And only then may we find
Some relief to our pain
The source of our pain is expansive
And the aftershocks great
Yet, even in our prayers,
We refuse to allow ourselves to be healed
A pain that flows with the blood in our veins
Feeling like little nerve pricks in our body
And not even a warm, loving touch can soothe us
One would think –
Just a slow release would cause some healing
But even the smallest outburst

Adds to the layers of anguish
Making each leakage feel like hot lava on the skin
Therefore, we refuse to share our pain
For fear of the scar
And, yet, when we look in the eyes of others
Our pain is reflected back
Causing us to hate our own image
So, we put on a smile and nod in silence.

No matter how deeply we cover the pain, the scars, and the hurt – it still exists. We were made to love. Love in truth when we love as God loves. Yet, we give up too easily. We look for the second or third chances, while struggling with unforgiveness and allow the pain to paralyze us from moving forward.

COMPLETE

An image formed out of complete nothingness
Exposing loneliness forever overlooked
It fills a void from deep inside
Causing a boil to rupture and flow
As it gently nurtures the crevices of the soul
Its silhouette casts a shadow over the entire being
Providing a sense of security, a sense of comfort
It's like a thirst long unfulfilled
A wound long forgotten about
The reflection of this image is an eclipse in motion
Only the goal is for ONE to remain over the other –
complete
Complete in quenching the thirst.
Complete in healing the wound.
Complete...complete...in love.

We must let God complete us. Truth is we are imperfect beings, incapable of perfect love. Nevertheless, there is One who loves us unconditionally with a perfect never-ending love. If we can get to the place, where we trust God for every encounter, for every pain, for every healing, we can experience true love and peace. When we can get to a place where we can love as God loves, we will find peace. We will have a heart without walls. We will experience healing.

If I am thankful for anything, it is for God's love that is beyond measure. A love that is full of grace. A love that forgives when I have trouble forgiving myself. A love that cleanses and heals when I feel used and abused. A love that fills me with hope when I don't see a reason to have hope. Even more, when I can't feel His love or hear His voice – I find a place of solitude and there I feel His warm love cover me and encourage me. Be encouraged… we are never alone in your pain and God heals all wounds.

Looking in the Rearview Mirror

Truth is healing is painful and often not immediate, yet necessary. As with most things, we can submit to the process or we can resist. Through resistance, I built walls of protection. I aimed to protect myself from all that would harm me. I placed my heart in a steel cage safe from all who sought me with false intentions, as if I knew *who* those people were.

I felt I had to shut off all feelings to keep from feeling. But how does a person know they are healing if they cannot feel? If the place that was once painful to touch now becomes numb – does that mean you are healed or that the feeling in that area is gone? We know that numbness in our limbs is not good. Not being able to feel our legs when touched is not a good sign. So why would we or I think having a heart that did not feel was good?

In contrast, sometimes we may find it more comforting to hold on to the pain as it has been with us for so long. I held some hurts for many years that they became a part of me. It was my comfort. The walls I built provided me with protection or so I perceived. I was able to walk around in hurt and gain sympathy for my pain.

Truth is by holding on to my pains and hurts, I wallowed in self-pity almost hoping others would feel pity for me also. Problem is all of this placed a focus on me and not God. As long as I held on to my pain, I could not heal. There are also many people who walk around smiling while dying inside – often hoping someone will recognize the hollowness inside. This is also not healing.

To heal, we must allow God's perfect work to have its way in us. Often He will heal parts of us and then take us to a deeper healing by helping us to rid ourselves of more pains from the past. The deeper He goes, the deeper we allow God to go, the deeper our healing.

Read: Proverbs 3:7-8, Matthew 6:22-23 and James 5:19-10

A Look in the Mirror　　　　　Date:

1. What baggage from previous relationships are you still carrying?

_____

_____

_____

_____

_____

_____

_____

2. What places in your heart remain unhealed?

_____

_____

_____

_____

_____

_____

_____

3. How have past relational hurts influenced how you engage with others today?

_____

_____

_____

_____

_____

_____

_____

God's Word:

"Is this not the fast that I have chosen: to loose the bonds of wickedness, to undo the heavy burdens, to let the oppressed go free, and that you break every yoke? Is it not to share your bread with the hungry, and that you bring to your house the poor who are cast out; When you see the naked, that you cover him, and not hide yourself from your own flesh? Then your light shall break forth like the morning, your healing shall spring forth speedily, and your righteousness shall go before you; The glory of the LORD shall be your rear guard. Then you shall call, and the LORD will answer; You shall cry, and He will say, 'Here I am.'" ~ Isaiah 58:6-9a

Prayer:

Lord, I thank You that You go before me and behind me. You encircle me and You hear me when I cry. I thank You for the healing You give in the midst of my pain. Your Word says that when I am faithful to You and help those who You bring to me, then You will be faithful to hear my prayers. Forgive me for the times when I can become so obsessed with my own issues that I lost focus of You. Forgive me for times of self-pity and self-loathing. I ask You, Father, to help me not be so focused on my pain, my issues, my hurts, my loss, that I lose focus on the purpose You have for me. In Jesus' Name, I pray. Amen.

Notes:

_____

_____

_____

_____

_____

_____

_____

_____

_____

_____

_____

_____

_____

_____

_____

_____

_____

_____

_____

_____

_____

_____

_____

_____

_____

_____

_____

_____

In The Wilderness

A CAGED BIRD

Like a caged bird, I long to be free
To break the chains of love
That inhibits my mind as well as my soul
To be released among the wilder
The ones who are seeking relief the same as I
Who are tired of burning tears
And unanswered prayers and hopeless dreams

To venture out without a thought of you
And our emotional bondage
You are beating me with those same tears in your eyes
Free me

Allow my heart to mend
My soul to mourn
All over the loss of love
Grant me my peace
To retreat within myself
Away from you and my soreness
Your pain hurts me even more
I want to be free

From the pain, the tears, the sadness
Even from the joy, the happiness and the love
Release me.

My prayers for many months were for the Lord to make my "husband" release me from the marriage. I just wanted to be free. I wanted to move on. I was also struggling with the thought of God wanting me to stay. I slowly realized I was getting nowhere fast. Suddenly, the place I was in felt familiar. I was wandering in a wilderness state – maturing.

I am no stranger to the desert. I have been there many times. Some short trips and some much longer than I would have wanted. I've be broken in the desert and rebuilt. I've suffered some of the hardest times of my life in the desert and yet celebrated some of my greatest victories there. I've gone to the desert kicking and screaming and other times I have found solace in the desert. One thing is for sure; God always meets me there. He is well prepared for my visit. He is the well-prepared host who has everything I need and things I don't know I need.

Yet, although I am familiar with the desert I somehow don't always realize immediately when I have arrived. I often miss the signs that show the changes in temperature and condition signaling the arrival to the dry place. Even in my despair, He is there. The desert is the place where He draws me away from all the chaos of the world so I can be with Him. So why do I resist it? It is often a place of solitude and quietness, a place of peace. A place of refreshing... Yet, my eyes only take in the barrenness, the uncertainty, and the place of wandering. I feel vulnerable and dread the attacks of the enemy, forgetting He is there. I feel unprotected, yet the desert is one of the most protected places because He is there with a purpose.

I know from experience that when I leave the desert I am more prepared for my next journey, yet, I fear it. I want to reach a place where I can welcome the desert as I would the change in seasons... Knowing that each season is needed and each has its own unique beauty and purpose.

So even though I know and am familiar with the desert experience, as I was faced with my new reality, I did not expect to leave my marriage situation and enter the desert. But that is where I landed. I went from a high of "I'm free!" to a "hold-up/not yet!" I thought by meeting the two other wives, my exit from the marriage would be easier and quicker, but that was not the case. It would be over a year before I was finally released from my mess.

I wandered around bitter and hurt in that wilderness, mad that God would not let me out. I was stuck. I wanted to be in the will of God and not the will of Danon but I also wanted to be free of this mess. I needed to hear from God. Did He, Almighty God, really want me to stay with this man? Maybe I was waiting for my "husband" to do the right thing. But surely God knew he would not – at least he hadn't up to this point. And why me? Why did I need to stay? What did God want me to learn? I just didn't understand. So I prayed even more for God to release me.

I got so fed up with my "husband" and his comfort level with the situation. This may have been the first time in a long while that he did not have to lie. Everything was out in the open. We all knew his mess. His goal was to get us to accept it. Two of us were not buying it, although he tried. He continued the lies as he determined who would actually keep him.

I tried to get an annulment, but since all the marriages happened in different states and countries, for that matter, I would need paperwork from the first marriage to prove he was married prior to me. I did not want a divorce. I wanted this marriage to never exist. The turmoil I felt when I attempted to file for divorce was so much that I stopped. The lawyer was awful. She blamed me. Then there was the expense of filing and how we would split our assets. The "splitting of assets" was the most unnerving, as he did not have anything! All that we had was mine. He had not worked. I had paid for everything. I had the most to lose. Nothing felt right and I did not understand why. I sought the peace I once felt. So I waited.

IN CONTEMPLATING

My petals have fallen
And are crushed by great feet
My leaves scrape to
Pull it all together

As my stem bends in the wind
The drops of rain
Are now puddles
Reflecting a broken soul

Deeper is vision
Of a once strong root
Protruding stem
With face open to the sky

The rays used to warm me
But now I am cold
My eyes shut tight
Preventing heat
While shivering from pain

Bent over, I see my roots
Escaping the ground
And I picture me
Flying through the sky

As I hold on with that last leg of mine
A horrifying thought crosses my mind
What if I do not fly free
But, yet, bump against the tress and ground
Only to be crushed
Again.

I recall telling this guy, who became attracted to me while I was going through all of this mess with my "husband", that God would not give him a married woman. The same was true in my situation. God would not have given me a married man nor would He have caused me to sin. I was in that situation because of my choices, because of my own sins. I chose to go my own way instead of choosing the Lord's way. I, in fact, created my own bed of suffering based on my decisions. God may have a husband for me but I chose the one I did. I couldn't blame God because I have free will and I moved forward even with all the warning signs.

I am a good example of what can happen when you don't seek and wait on the Lord for guidance and direction. I found myself between a rock and a hard place. I had my vows, my covenant to God, or divorce. It was like sin got me into this relationship and I considered sin to get me out. I saw divorce as sin...a breaking of my covenant with God. I knew God would not require me to stay based on my "husband's" actions. I also knew I could not move ahead of God. I had to allow His timing and His way. God's Word says, "The temptations in your life are no different from what others experience. And God is faithful. He will not allow the temptation to be more than you can stand. When you are tempted, He will show you a way out so that you can endure" (1 Corinthians 10:13 NLT version).

It is truly difficult to look around and see yourself in a bad situation because of your own sin and disobedience. I had to acknowledge this was not something I could get out of alone. I needed God more than ever to help me and lead me. I had to get to a point where I truly gave up and asked God to take control of my mess! I had to allow His work in me to be completed at His pace. This was not easy for me at all.

I had to admit I was not happy with God. I knew He had the power to release me from this marriage. He could change my "husband's heart", granted my "husband" would need to be willing since we all have free will. Truth is, I looked back on the night of his illness before our marriage, and many times as I struggled and wondered why God did not take him then – knowing what He knew. Maybe God was giving him another chance to make things right. Maybe God was answering my prayers and giving me the desires of my heart. I don't really know why God let him live but I had to trust His wisdom.

I walked aimlessly around the wilderness searching for the reason God would not release me. I closed myself off from everyone. I did not want to hear those on my side or those on his side. The only words I wanted to receive in my life were those of God. If what I heard could not be verified by God's Word, I rejected it. God then placed women in my life who were after His own heart, and through them, He spoke to me. God used these women to answer things I'd never spoken to anyone but Him. I submitted to God. I decided to be still while allowing God to work on me. So I waited and sought God for my way out.

I committed to release my need to control the seasons... my need to know (period) and submitted to trusting in Him. Trusting in His timing, in His protection, in His wisdom, and in His love for me. Truth is He is Always faithful and is always there prepared for my desert time.... Thus, I submitted to resting in Him for as long as He had me there. I gave up my desires and began to seek His. I found Him to be faithful and loving beyond my comprehension. I allowed myself to trust Him because He had proven Himself faithful.

It was at that point when I took my eyes off me and started to look at my husband as God showed him to me that my prayers changed. I began to pray for my "husband" as if he truly were my husband. I wanted him healed. I wanted him delivered and not just for me but for him. I truly wanted him saved. I felt my purpose in the wilderness was to lift him in prayer. I slowly realized I had been praying for selfish motives.

I started to understand the purpose of my wilderness visit. I started to learn my lesson. I also realized that my covenant to God would not be broken when I divorced this man, I realized that it was broken when I first sinned. James 1:14 states, "Temptation comes from our own desires, which entice us and drags us away." I was "dragged away" when I first stepped outside of God's will and allowed my flesh to rule me and when I first stopped seeking God and acted on my own emotions. So the marriage was a covenant I made that was not aligned to God's will and was out of disobedience to Him. It is only His grace that would set me free from my sins!

.

Looking in the Rearview Mirror

Sometimes God takes us to the wilderness so we can hear Him better... other times, we push ourselves there through our actions and choices. No matter how we get there, God is often waiting for us and He is always with us. Once there, we often make our own tracks around the mountain. The number of laps often depends on how well we learn the lessons being taught.

Deuteronomy 8:2 says, "Remember how the Lord your God led you through the wilderness for these forty years, humbling you and testing you to prove your character, and to find out whether or not would obey His commands." God seeks to strengthen us through our wilderness experience. If we follow the journey of the Israelites, God provided for them, protected them and went before them. The wilderness is a time of separation... often a time of clarity. Yet, it is full of the unknown.

We have to know we cannot rush the "wilderness" time. We have to be open to learning and pruning. For me, it is a reminder that I am not in control of the seasons. I can only control how I move through the seasons. Do I move anxiously? Do I move begrudgingly? Do I despise the extremes of cold and hot? Or do I seek to enjoy every minute knowing each is full of purpose?

In my wilderness, I would be patient at times – or what I thought was patient. Many times, I was anxiously screaming for the desert time to be over. Yet, God was patiently testing and building my character. God wanted to see if I would give up on Him and do my own thing, once again, or if I truly would follow Him.

What do you think God is asking of you? Think of your wilderness times. How have you responded?

I have come to a place where when I recognize I am in the wilderness, I stop fighting and sit to learn. I don't want to add to my laps around the mountain. I want to be humble to the process and be obedient to God's will in my life.

Read: Philippians 4:6-7, Psalm 78:39-41 and Isaiah 43:18-20 & 48:21

A Look in the Mirror   Date:

1. When was your last wilderness experience?

_____
_____
_____
_____
_____
_____
_____

2. What have you learned from your wilderness experience?

_____
_____
_____
_____
_____
_____
_____

3. When have you tried to move ahead of God's timing? What has been the result?

_____
_____
_____
_____
_____
_____
_____

God's Word:

"Trust God from the bottom of your heart; don't try to figure out everything on your own. Listen for God's voice in everything you do, everywhere you go; He's the One who will keep you on track. Don't assume that you know it all. Run to God! Run from evil! Your body will glow with health, your very bones will vibrate with life! Honor God with everything you own; give Him the first and the best. Your barns will burst, your wine vats will brim over. But don't, dear friend, resent God's discipline; don't sulk under His loving correction. It's the child He loves that He corrects; a father's delight is behind all this." ~ Proverbs 3:5-12 (The Message version)

Prayer:

Father, I confess I don't always like the wilderness. I don't have the patience often needed to let You be God. Help me to trust You more. Help me to not try to figure everything out but to trust that You have me. You have my future. And Your love for me is perfect. Your ways are perfect. I choose to trust You even when I don't understand. I choose to put You first and honor You in all I do. I thank You for your correction as that reflects Your love for me and deep desire for me to prosper in all that You have for me. Father, guide me and lead me through the uncertainties of life. In Jesus' Name, I pray. Amen.

Notes:

_____

_____

_____

_____

_____

_____

_____

_____

_____

_____

_____

_____

_____

_____

_____

_____

_____

_____

_____

_____

_____

_____

_____

_____

_____

_____

_____

_____

I Pray For You

See, I thought my prayers were for you and how you
should be
And how God should cover you and even bless you
I thought in my prayers I was praying for you
For your forgiveness and direction
For your feet to be planted firmly
But God is good all the time
HE will bring the truth to light
And in HIS love, HE showed me - me

So, as I prayed to God to guide you, be there for you
The negative feelings did not leave
I prayed for God's grace to cover you and for the evil
spirits to leave
Yet, I felt no peace
I prayed to God to deliver you from your situation and
give you peace, too
Still I burned inside from the pain
Then God spoke to me and showed me the pain I had
caused
And how in my actions I hurt HIM by my disobedience
My lack or repentance, my selfishness, my blindness to
my own actions
HE showed me how not forgiving was a sin

HE showed me my bitterness, my judgment of you
HE showed me how I spoke of forgiveness but did not
live it
And as I thought you were the person to change my life
from good to bad
HE showed me HE is in control and it is not all about
ME

HE showed me my pride and negativity
My sins were brought to light, no longer hidden
In HIS love I found myself bare, as I prayed for you…

I repented
I looked away in tears
And there the light shined on the truth in my life
I was not just praying for you and those who wronged me
I was praying for me
I was praying for God to guide me in HIS path
I was praying to hear God's voice softly on my ear
I was praying for forgiveness of my sins and my negative attitude
I was praying for God's grace to cover me
I was crying out to the Lord to touch me with HIS love
Allow me to see those I have wronged
Allow me to see where my faith has faltered
Give me eyes so I can see, and ears so I can hear
Teach me to be an Abraham, David, Job, Mary, Ruth, or even Paul
Teach me to be more like Jesus in every facet possible
And help me to pray for me.

Break Me!

I want to be broken
So I can be used by You
I know in my wholeness
I am too secure in me

I want to be broken of pride
Of being too full of me
I want to be broken of fear
Thinking it is all about me
I want to be broken of anger
Being too controlled by my rage
I want to be broken of lust
Allowing my flesh to control my thoughts
I want to be broken of depression and sadness
Trapped in the emptiness of my mind

Lord, I know if I am broken by You
You will make me whole
You satisfy the deep yearnings of my heart
You provide peace in the midst of the storm
You guide my feet though the darkness
You settle my mind when it is out of control
You make a way when there is no way
You give joy that is beyond my understanding

Fill me, Lord, with more of You
Break me and remake me
Lord, when I am broken, You Are!!!

Once, I fully submitted to God, I submitted to the process. I allowed myself to be broken. I stopped fighting the pain. I stopped dwelling on being in the wilderness. I stopped asking how it would end and focused on the moment where He had me. I allowed His way in my life, which often meant facing my brokenness in places I was not fully aware.

The first thing I had to be broken of was my feelings of rejection. Rejection hurts, no matter how innocently done. I know because I had been rejected many times and I am sure I have rejected others. It is hard to say when one rejection may have hurt more than another. The rejection from this man believed to be my husband seemed to top the list.

It may be because my love that was offered so openly, so sincerely was crushed and thrown back at me. My vulnerabilities were used against me. I trusted and had that trust destroyed. It was like going into a haunted house and learning nothing was as it seemed. Things change. People change. Sometimes people are not who they profess to be. For me, my picture was continually changed, destroyed and never rebuilt to the beauty it was once imagined to be.

Sometimes in being rejected, we can fall into denial. Rather, we are in denial on how things really are. Maybe my picture always looked as ugly as it looked now and I thought a pretty frame would make it look better. That was so not the case.

In the end, I believe I was attracted to rejection. I felt I must look for it and yearn for it since that was what I constantly sought in relationships. I went through all of those emotions to realize God would never reject me. He never has and never will. I may have rejected Him and His guidance but God is not like man. My faith has wavered and my hope had dried up. I felt worthy of nothing or little and therefore I sought little, thus seeking rejection. Once I allowed God to heal me of rejection and receive His acceptance, I was on to the next stage of my brokenness for healing.

I found I was holding out for my "husband" to do the right thing. I am not sure why I thought that was possible, as he had not done the "right" thing up to that point. See, he knew the bible. He could recite scriptures and preach a message… he just did not walk the message. I had looked to him as the spiritual leader in our marriage and he was far from that. I had depended on his understanding of the bible instead of seeking that understanding for myself. God was teaching me that I needed to have a personal relationship with Him and know Him for myself.

I must admit being broken can be painful. During this time, I held on to two scriptures: Proverbs 3:5-6, "Trust in the Lord with all your heart and lean not on your own understanding. In your ways acknowledge Him and He will direct your paths." This scripture reminded me to stop asking to understand the situation and to continually turn my focus to the Lord. Romans 8:28 reminded me that God is in control. The enemy will not win. I rested in those scriptures.

I saw a quote once that read, "God is still God, even when things don't go your way." I found this is what it means to "trust" God. This is the ability to trust God regardless of the outcome, regardless of the situation, regardless of our needs, wants, desired, etc. It is about releasing the need to control. Even for those who are highly intelligent, we all have to recognize we don't know everything.

I didn't know why God let my "husband" live that night during our honeymoon, but He did. And I am sure he let him live as much for him as it was for me. I know His ways are perfect. The testing ground is that place where you still trust Him even when you don't understand. It is about trusting God above my own ways. I cannot allow my sorrow or loss or the way I feel to be above or higher than God's ways. I can never get to a place where I feel I know better than God what is best in my life or the lives of others.

James 1:2 states, "Consider it pure joy, my brothers, whenever you face trials of many kinds, because you know that the testing of your faith develops perseverance." The truth is we typically don't find "joy" in our trials. We focus on the moment, the here and now, not how this particular trial strengthens our faith. Everyone faces difficulties and at times, we may feel our difficulty is worse than someone else's, but it is ours. A difficulty specifically made for us to develop the perseverance we need to "mature and complete". Interestingly, the trials I need to complete me may not be the same ones you need to complete you. My "trials" during this season definitely strengthened my faith.

Another area of brokenness God showed me was I allowed my flesh to rule my thoughts and me. I did not have the mind of Christ. If it felt right, I went with it. My thoughts blocked the words of Christ. I wanted to be loved and I wanted a marriage so much so that my thoughts were consumed with this. I held on way past the expiration date of a relationship. Then in light of the pain I felt, it seemed easier to live without love than live with it. Daily we are subjected to things that can cause our belief in love to fail. In my flesh, I am not always the best person to love or give love in return. I want and need to believe that there is something good in me.... That God can find a place to reside in me, in all of my mess. That He loves me enough to save me or rather that I am not so messed up that He has lost hope in me. See, if I thought with my mind, I would never feel the presence of the Lord as my mind was overwhelmed with thoughts of my flesh. With my "husband" I was still waiting on him to make a decision when in actuality, his decision was made by his actions. At this point, I wasn't totally healed of my brokenness, only aware of the impact of my thought life.

I felt pain today
There, in my missing limb
I know it's gone
But it still hurts
I still see it there
I still feel it there
I cry from the pain and confusion
Knowing it shouldn't bother me
Now that it's gone
I don't know if it's
Because I wish it back or if I just hadn't let it go
But it's still here with me... Mentally
And I guess I feel pain
Because physically it isn't

Always remember God is never surprised by a situation in our lives – either by our own choosing or by plans of the enemy. God sees out life in its entirety – not just parts but from before our conception to the end of our life here on earth. God makes a way out of every situation and His plans for our life are perfect. Our challenge is to be obedient and submit to His will.

I continually wanted to tell God what was happening to me; what my "husband" had done to me and these other women. Slowly, I realized God is God... He already knew this before it happened. I was having a conversation with God over my situation and God told me to look at Him – keep my focus on Him and I would not fall. It's like Peter walking on water towards Jesus,

Peter was fine till he looked down and realized the miracle of what was happening. This... my situation was not a surprise to God. He already had a way out for me.

Having this faith, this trust in God is about being still, having faith and allowing God to be God. We don't have to row the boat anywhere – unless God says to. Just be still and allow God to be God. Have faith that God is in control – All the Time! It is funny how this works. I have checked myself at times and said, "OK, I am not going to worry about this. I am responsible to God for my actions. Then when I was still – not trying to be God– I saw God working some things out. I can't say I knew His plan but I know His work.

We have to trust God more than we trust ourselves and God will show up. After my failed relationships - I was (finally) at the point where I could say – I don't trust Danon to determine my relationships. I trust God. He alone knows the beginning and the end. Thus, I have to trust God for a mate. I pray often to desire only what God desires for me. I only want what God wants for me. So even with a man, I pray for God to work – move away those who are not in God's plan for me and prepare me for the man He has reserved for me. I don't want to act on flesh and I don't want Danon to be in control.

I have to say, I have learned the hard way about what happens when I act on my own. "Two shall become one". This is such a profound statement and promise, yet, many times we miss out on God's promises because we have moved without Him. I wanted to become one with my ex, yet, I became 1/3 of the whole. From that day on, I vowed to keep my eyes on God and where they belonged.

I strived to trust God more and more. Once I submitted and allowed God's will to be done, things

turned out much better than I could have ever planned. I
initially sought a divorce and then an annulment. God
gave me a void to my marriage! That meant it never
existed!!! I was ecstatic. I could actually say I was
"never" married. I loved it! How did God work this out?
Well, the first wife got a divorce. She sent me an email
to tell me about it. I found out the date of the divorce and
pulled up the divorce certificate online. My new attorney
used that to obtain a "void" on my marriage! God
worked it out in His timing!

Looking in the Rearview Mirror

Often, we have to be broken of the past. Broken from the pain. Broken from hurts and hang-ups. But we tend to fight the brokenness, thinking we can heal ourselves. But God is the One who heals. His Word says we should be like clay in the Potter's hands.

"God told Jeremiah, "Up on your feet! Go to the potter's house. When you get there, I'll tell you what I have to say." So I went to the potter's house, and sure enough, the potter was there, working away at his wheel. Whenever the pot the potter was working on turned out badly, as sometimes happens when you are working with clay, the potter would simply start over and use the same clay to make another pot. Then God's Message came to me: "Can't I do just as this potter does, people of Israel?" God's Decree! "Watch this potter. In the same way that this potter works his clay, I work on you, people of Israel. At any moment I may decide to pull up a people or a country by the roots and get rid of them. But if they repent of their wicked lives, I will think twice and start over with them. At another time I might decide to plant a people or country, but if they don't cooperate and won't listen to me, I will think again and give up on the plans I had for them" (Jeremiah 18:1-10, The Message version).

Submitting to be broken is not an easy task. You have to trust the Potter. God knows best and will help to mold you into a wholeness that will accomplish His plans for you. We often resist the breaking down and the pain of remolding but the outcome is far better than our original state.

When we reach a place where we admit we are no longer happy with the way we are and choose to submit to being broken, then God can have His way with us. The difference with healing and brokenness is God uses the healing to cleanse and the brokenness to rebuild.

I feel the need to remind you that hindsight is

20/20 vision. Everything is always much clearer once you have passed it. You are able to see with a different set of eyes. You have a different revelation then you did while you were in the moment. Thus, don't harp on your mistakes of the past. Allow God to break you down and rebuild you into His masterpiece creation.

Read: Psalm 51:17, Ezekiel 34:15-17, Isaiah 48:6-8

A Look in the Mirror   **Date:**

1. How do you deal with rejection?

_____
_____
_____
_____
_____
_____
_____

2. What do you think the Lord wants to break in you?

_____
_____
_____
_____
_____
_____
_____

3. Do you have anyone with whom you could share your greatest fears and pains?

_____
_____
_____
_____
_____
_____
_____

God's Word:

> "But now, O LORD, You are our Father; We are the clay, and You our potter; And we are the work of Your hand." ~ Isaiah 64:8

> "The word which came to Jeremiah from the LORD, saying: 'Arise and go down to the potter's house, and there I will cause you to hear My words.' Then I went down to the potter's house, and there he was, making something at the wheel. And the vessel that he made of clay was marred in the hard of the potter; so he made it again into another vessel, as it seemed good to the potter to make." ~ Jeremiah 18:1-4

Prayer:

> Father, I thank You that you break me to remake me in Your image. Please break off everything that is not of You. Help me to see myself as You see me and see those things that are not of You. Show me the marred parts of me that I may willingly submit to the process to be re-made. I ask this in Jesus' Name. Amen.

Notes:

_____
_____
_____
_____
_____
_____
_____
_____
_____
_____
_____
_____
_____
_____
_____
_____
_____
_____
_____
_____
_____
_____
_____
_____
_____
_____
_____
_____

A New Direction

I awoke this morning and felt
A new direction
A change – whether for the best or worst
I welcome it
I felt new energies
Arise inside of me
A voice calling
Relieving me of my worries
Taking me on a journey
In silence I followed
I took in freely
The pleasures of the world
And marveled at its beauty
I felt so overwhelmed
By its mere innocence
Every event during the day
Came with reason and purpose
But I was like a leaf
Floating in the stream
Carelessly being carried away
I thought today
About my life
Its pains but mostly its pleasures
I took an unspoken vow
To let things be
I thought of Him today
And the warmth of Him in me
I thought of me also
Of my wants, my judgments, hesitancy
I thought of a path I may take
To find serenity and fullness
And I rose

I laid my miseries and worries
In the hands of the Lord
We spoke no dialogue – not a word
He just picked them up
And took my hand
I feel comfort in His guidance
It's a new direction
And I'm following wherever He leads me

I'm Ready!

"Lord, I'm ready!" That is what I said during worship one night. I threw my hands in the air and surrendered to His will. Hands wide open and heart ready to receive. I am ready! I may have hemmed and hawed but now, I am ready to stop dragging my feet. I have sat around and got some things accomplished but have taken it all in stride, no rush. I have asked for time to digest things and decide how I want to handle them, but now I am ready!

Ready for what? Ready to walk into the next season God has for me. Often times, we are our own delay. We hold on to things of the past and drag our feet when it is time to move forward. We procrastinate or deliberate when we can just drop it all and make forward strides. Now, I have had a good season of growth and learning but I have also enjoyed my rest. I have deliberated on moving forward to ensure I was ready. I tried at a time to rush some things, but only things I felt needed to be rushed. God would not be rushed!

Funny thing, He is often waiting on us to be ready. Ready to move. Ready to act. Ready to forgive. Ready to love. Ready to heal. Yet, we have to be ready for something new. We can get so accustomed to a condition that something new can be scary. I was finally able to say I forgave my ex. I was finally able to pray for him without feeling any hurt or anger. I truly want him healed and whole. I know if he turns to God, God can use him to save other souls. Yes, he finally gave up contacting me – at least I haven't heard from him in a few years. I don't believe he is still with the 3rd wife, as he shared at one time she was unhappy with him and may have even put him in jail for a stint. I pray she has forgiven him also.

> *There is freedom in forgiveness*
> *Power in letting go*
> *No more emotional attachment*
> *Over what you did to me and I to you*
> *The destructive path is gone*
> *Healing has come*
> *Who knew all the places*
> *Made dark by my unforgiveness?*
> *Healing has come*
> *No more bitterness, no more regrets*
> *I see you through God's eyes*
> *And you are beautiful...*
> *Now that I have forgiven*

I've also learned the importance and value of having accountability partners. People who love me and are honest with me and will correct me, as needed. This is a safe guard for me and for you also, if you have friends who can hold you accountable. If I truly want God's best for me, I have to trust God and walk in His ways. I cannot walk the fence between right and wrong. I can't choose what I think is "good" based on how I feel. And I cannot operate my life in darkness. I have to be willing and open to have my life examined.

Once you surrender to God and allow Him to take control, there becomes a new adventure. Once you realize you don't have to do it alone, God is with you. God's love is perfect. He does not love like man does. God does not lie. And He can make you well, if you are willing. And God's plans for you are also perfect. You enter a new type of freedom when you place your trust and your life in God. So, are you ready? I pray you will find that place of full surrender and allow God to lead you into His Presence and cover you in His perfect peace and love.

Afterthought

My experiences in this book took a few years. It took me many years to heal. I say this because I do not want anyone to think healing was instantaneous. I was stuck in my "marriage" for 3.5 years before God released me. Give yourself grace and be forgiving of yourself. We all make mistakes and it may be longer of shorter before we realize we are in a mess. But know that God is able to turn any situation around. He can restore. He can heal. He can mend. Trust Him. He is already aware of your situation and circumstances and does not love you any less by knowing. Seek His wisdom for your situation, for your life. Trust Him. He loves you with an everlasting love.

Feel His Love

There is release in loving You
Release from the past and release into the future
The unknown... at least to me
God knows
There is acceptance in all of this
Acceptance that I am not in control
But the One who knows is in control
And I trust HIM over me
To love you is to reflect God's grace
Even as I am undeserving, there is HIS love
Showering me with an undeserving kindness
I walk an unchartered path for me

Journey with me for a moment
See the beauty God has created in Love
God is in Love
And to know Love is a Blessing
Yet, a blessing so rare in true form
It's not the lies, fears, loneliness, and desires
Mistaken for love
There is nothing more perfect
Than the love from God
A love woven through trust
The kind where you open your arms wide
And fall back... Knowing you won't fall
It's to travel to a place thought out of reach

Imagine streams flowing in several directions
All away from you
Yet, with just a thought of thirst
The stream turns to you
Filling you from the inside out

See, My God knows your needs
And fills them even before you think it
HE sees the end,
Yet, meets you right where you are
HIS love is
More than we could ever dream
And when we thought love was beyond repair
He saw wholeness renewed
Maybe I am just in love with God's love
Amazing love full of HIS Grace
Healing, refreshing, comforting and fulfilling
I stand
Awaiting His next move
Yet, all that is required of me is an open heart
A heart I thought was forever broken

Acknowledgments

I have so much to be thankful for and so many to thank. First and foremost, I give all the glory and praise to Jehovah God almighty. God carried me through the darkness of my life and loved me through my mess. When I turned my back on Him, He still loved me back to Him. God brought me to Texas, a place that haunted me as a child, and redeemed this place for me. He brought godly women into my life that loved me through my pain and shame. Yes, I owe this book to Him and it is because of God that I am able to share my story in hopes that someone else experiences His healing grace.

I am so thankful to my Covenant Church family. My first Life Team Leader, LaKendria King and the women in that group showed me the love of God I had never experienced. They allowed me to expose the wounds of my heart for the first time without fear of rejection or shame. LaKendria also taught me how to be a good small group leader. My sisters in Christ: Jackie Shepherd, Sherri Lee, Charis Powell - my Jamaican friend, Robyn Taylor, Patrice, Frenzetta Speed, Sandei Struebing, Stephany Lewis-Diaz, Deena Lopez, and all the ladies in my small group: *Women Trusting in God...* I love you and I thank God for each of you. You each hold a special place in my heart. I am eternally grateful for your support, encouragement, and praying me through my healing process. God truly blessed me with these relationships.

Suad Asselin, my photographer and cover designer whose talents are just amazing... thank you my friend for your artist ability blessed by God! Look her up at suadphotography.com! And my brother, Leon for your creativity and web design work. I love you and thanks for always being there for me!

I am thankful to my Sorors, Alicia Procello Maddox, Nikki Alexander, and Asani Charles, who were with me through my mess and gave me a shoulder to cry on. Thank you ladies for standing with me and sticking with me through the healing process… your prayers and words of encouragement helped me through my most difficult times.

And to my biggest cheerleaders – my family… I could not have made it without your support and unconditional love. My son, Zaire, my Grammie and Grandpa, my brothers, Leon and Kenyan, and my favorite sister, Cuqui, all my aunts and uncles and cousins… I wouldn't trade you for the world! Family means everything to me. I love you more!

22311105R00089

Made in the USA
San Bernardino, CA
01 July 2015